SABETH RUNDLE CHARLES

An Invitation

SATISFIED

rd Higashi

Loving Desperation

REJOICE

illiam Spencer Walton

CAPTIVE HEART

idden Pearls

A Special Gift

FOR: ....

FROM: ....

DATE: ....

....

ISBN: 1-59475-013-0

Cover/Interior: Synnöve Inman Design

Contributing Editors: James G. Waldrup III, William C. Bean, Gary William Evans & Virginia M. Davis

Research Editors: Elizabeth W. Bidwell & Jennifer Andrada

Published by Blue Sky Ink, a division of GRQ Ink, Brentwood, Tennessee 37024

Printed in China.

BLUE
SKY
INK

BRENTWOOD
TENNESSEE

HIDDEN PEARLS

COME AND REJOICE

COME AND REJOICE

Table of Contents

LIKE PRECIOUS PEARLS HIDDEN IN THE DEEP,

MANY HYMNS STILL LINGER WITHIN

THE INSPIRED AND LIFE-GIVING TREASURY

OF SACRED SONG, WAITING TO

BE ENJOYED BY GOD'S PEOPLE.

NOT CREATED TO BE FORGOTTEN,

THESE GEMS OF ETERNAL VALUE TRULY REFLECT

CHRIST'S RADIANT FACE FOR ALL TO SEE.

Discover Hidden Pearls

Be filled with the Spirit, speaking to one another in psalms and
hymns and spiritual songs. *Ephesians 5:18b–19a*

Let the word of Christ dwell in you richly in all wisdom,
teaching and admonishing one another in psalms and hymns and spiritual songs,
singing with grace in your hearts to the Lord. *Colossians 3:16*

SPEAKING THE TRUTH—
SINGING WITH GRACE

As the oyster organically applies the pearly transforming element to its wound,
a solid gem of beauty and worth is created for others to enjoy.
Likewise, the most excellent of spiritual poems are created where divine grace
has mingled with man's frailty in the crucible of human experience.
Such poems can be compared to lustrous pearls that
brightly portray the hidden life of the oysters that produce them.
Both the poets and their poetic pearls are an expression of God's metamorphic work.

From the first century, countless lovers of the Lord Jesus Christ have crystallized their deepest sentiments and sweetest appreciation of things divine into song. The Word richly indwelling the first Christians flowed into poetic verse—spoken and sung—and served as a means to preserve and convey the critical messages of the Faith. Their scriptural practice of speaking the truth to one another and singing with grace to the Lord established the standard of spiritual music for all generations. Indeed, the songs of faith should be saturated with truth, rich in detail, and experiential in nature. Such songs tune our hearts to the divine realities that exist in the spiritual realm for our guidance and enjoyment. Accordingly, we are inspired to give glory to God, speak encouragement to men, and heap shame on the tempter.

Our privilege at *Hidden Pearls Publishing* is to present life-changing messages from those who have gone before us. This exceptional treasury of hymns includes authors whose diversity extends beyond historic period, geography, culture, and social status. Yet, in one harmonic voice, they lift up the radiant beauty of the Savior for all to see. As grapes sub-

Discover Hidden Pearls

mitting to the winepress of circumstance, their lives through Christ were voluntarily poured out for our benefit. These authors exemplify people who loved God, sought truth, denied themselves, and explored the divine mysteries. Through their lives, we glimpse the spiritual heritage of the church that has always faithfully, accurately, and lovingly ministered Christ. Thus, we are compelled to present their stories!

But their stories would be incomplete without the music that brings their poetry to life. As lovely pearls deserve an elegant setting, so these lyrics are also worthy to be presented within the nobility of classic instrumentation and sung with the voices of appreciating hearts. To that end, *Hidden Pearls Publishing* has recorded these songs with the finest arrangements and full symphonic orchestration, available on companion CDs. It is our utmost desire to deliver these hymns in faithfulness to their message; therefore, we pray for guidance and labor for excellence.

May the Lord multiply His blessing of these hymns, devotions, and stories for the nourishment of the entire Christian community and beyond. We invite you to come and enjoy their fellowship in this never-ending divine romance between God and His people.

From the Editors of Hidden Pearls

Discover Hidden Pearls

An Invitation

The immediate result of the coming of

these good tidings of great joy to me

was no outward change in anything,

but an inward change of everything.

Elisabeth Rundle Charles

Come and Rejoice with Me!

ELISABETH RUNDLE CHARLES
1828–1896

An Invitation to the Christian Life

And the Spirit and the bride say, "Come!" And let him who hears say, "Come!"
And let him who thirsts come. Whoever desires, let him take the water of life freely. (Revelation 22:17)

For the bread of God is He who comes
down from heaven and gives life to the world. (John 6:33)

What words could portray the sweet, open, and welcoming invitation of the Christian life more aptly than these: "Come and rejoice with me! For I have found a Friend." Through this poem, Elisabeth Rundle Charles simply and wondrously describes her joyful discovery of the One Who came down out of heaven freely inviting all to come and feast on Him as bread divine. By enjoying God's free gift of grace, we taste something of heaven's life on earth.

"Come and rejoice with me! For I was wearied sore." Upon finding Him, there is no longer the need to restlessly wander or wistfully wonder, "What is the meaning of life?" He is our satisfaction and the answer to our every problem. Do we need love? He is "a treasury of love, a boundless store." Do we need a friend? He is One "Who knows my heart's most secret depths, yet loves me without end!"

Christ the Lord Himself has drawn close enough for us to experience Him directly, personally, and intimately. For us to live pleasingly and joyfully before God, there is no substitute for the enabling supply that flows from Him to us. In the realm of things truly Christian—Christ is everything!

Yes, we may rejoice, for by the Father's wise design, His Son Jesus Christ is perfectly suited to meet our every need—and more than sufficiently so! Let us attend to that welcoming voice of invitation to come and rejoice in Christ, Who is a treasury of richest delights!

Come and Rejoice with Me!

Come and Rejoice with Me!

Verse One

Come and rejoice with me!
For once my heart was poor,
And I have found a treasury
Of love, a boundless store.

Verse Two

Come and rejoice with me!
I, once so sick at heart,
Have met with One Who knows my case,
And knows the healing art.

Verse Three

Come and rejoice with me!
For I was wearied sore,
And I have found a mighty arm
Which holds me evermore.

Verse Four

Come and rejoice with me!
My feet so wide did roam,
And One has brought me from afar,
To find in Him my home.

Verse Five

Come and rejoice with me!
For I have found a Friend
Who knows my heart's most secret depths,
Yet loves me without end.

Verse Six

I knew not of His love;
And He had loved so long,
With love so faithful and so deep,
So tender and so strong.

Verse Seven

And now I know it all,
Have heard and known His voice,
And hear it still from day to day.
Can I enough rejoice?

COME AND REJOICE WITH ME!

An Invitation to the Christian Life

FACTORY'S GRIND ALTERS NATURE'S RHYTHM

Within one generation, society in England was transformed from rural and agrarian to urban and industrial. Factory workers were considered to have less intrinsic value than what they built and maintained and were treated as mere expendable cogs in factory machinery. Pay was so low that parents sent their children, with their useful small hands, to work for family survival. Fresh air and sunshine had been replaced by the stench of relentless, pluming gray smoke from kerosene lamps and coal-fired furnaces. Poverty, squalor, sickness, and misery prevailed, all to make production, communication, and transportation faster and more efficient. Amid this suffering, Elisabeth Rundle Charles gave her whole life to pour out the Lord's love in word and deed to those surrounding her, both rich and poor.

On a crisp autumn day near the end of the nineteenth century in rural southwest England, Elisabeth Rundle Charles stood on the crest of a hill overlooking the village of Morwellham on the river Tamar. The shipping wharves had fallen into disrepair, but the river still flowed like a winding bright blue ribbon to the sea. As Elisabeth shaded her eyes from the setting sun, the abundant recollections from her heart began to pour forth, for it was also the sunset of her life.

Fifty years before, the region below presented a different scene. On either side of the bustling river "rose hills clothed with woods," and at the base of the hills lay "treasure heaps of copper ore." Today, no ships were on the river, the wooded hills were cut bare, and the treasure heaps where she had played with her cousins in her happy childhood were gone. But what a picturesque and encompassing vista she remembered. From the lovely, safe sanctuary of her early years, her life had flourished like a flowing river across the land in which she became famous and renowned as one of England's great writers, historians, and linguists. Her Christian voice spoke eloquently through her fifty published books. Elisabeth's thoughts wandered from both the pleasant memories of her childhood and

Simply Hearing His Voice

GOD HIMSELF IS NEARER US THAN ANY OF THE CREATURES OR CIRCUMSTANCES THROUGH WHICH HE MOVES US; SINCE *INBREATHING* IS A FINER EXPRESSION OF HIS WORK IN US THAN IMPELLING; AND SINCE EVERY GOOD AND TRUE WORK ... IS INSPIRED BY THE SPIRIT OF GOD.

ERC

Come and Rejoice with Me!

the comparative emptiness of the scene before her, to thoughts of "a higher sense," to "a far higher life beyond our sight and hearing." To know her life is to understand the meaning of her thoughts.

A SENSE THAT GOD WAS THERE

Elisabeth grew up in nearby Tavistock, but the Rundle family often spent summer months in the village of Morwellham, where many of the family businesses were located. Her childhood was serene and delightful. Her father, John Rundle, was a highly respected man of integrity, intelligence, and unselfishness. He was a banker, a member of Parliament, a community employer, and a respected leader whose benevolence blessed many through times of great need and unrest. And he was Elisabeth's closest friend. Her mother, Joana, provided a well-ordered and peaceful home with a "quiet pervading presence, a sweet brooding, a sunny warmth." Indeed, this precious atmosphere of childhood nurturing and safekeeping was a reference point across Elisabeth's whole life.

Elisabeth, though an only child, was raised and educated alongside her cousins, with whom she shared a closeness like that among loving sisters. They were educated by governesses who creatively immersed them in global geography, history, and math. Later, tutors trained them in the classic disciplines of algebra, composition, and the languages of Latin, Greek, Italian, French, and German. There were also "sojourns in London, during the Parliamentary Session," and she traveled throughout England, France, and Germany in her youth.

Moreover, Elisabeth's spiritual environment had been full of God's love. There were prayers at her mother's bedside and the singing of old hymns of Cowper, the Wesleys, and Watts, "dimly understood, but flowing with a sense of music through the heart." She speaks of a "sense that God was there and ready to bless and help me and mine."

Yet, in the midst of this idyllic life of love and learning, the mercy of God came to Elisabeth so that she might learn of her fundamental and acute need of Him.

⌒⌒⌒⋇⌒⌒⌒

"EUREKA!" "I HAVE FOUND HIM"

In her teenage years, Elisabeth aspired to the "high and beautiful ideal of Christian life and character." She longed for "the stamp of the faith" to be "visible everywhere and at all times," not banished "to a corner of the week or of the world." Yet, through observation of the "divided and distracted family [of God's children], scarcely one of which seemed on speaking terms with the others," Elisabeth became increasingly disillusioned with the spiritual condition of the church in general. Furthermore, upon looking within herself, she acknowledged in despair that instead of seeing the ideal in her own heart, she saw a completely "unsatisfactory self." With this illumination "came the pain of the terrible rendings and ruin of this ideal, without; the weariness of the failure to reach the ideal, within." This deepening sense of hopelessness within herself and others drove her to find a remedy.

Though "weeks of distress and conflict followed" in Elisabeth's search for reality, the One Who knew her case faithfully continued the work of revelation within her. When she was eighteen, He sent César Malan, a Swiss acquaintance, to speak to her "simply of the immeasurable and unmerited love of God." One lovely, sunny afternoon, as they were walking down an avenue lined with beech trees, Malan shared timeless truths with Elisabeth:

He spoke ... of the burden of sin borne away by the Redeemer, the Lamb of God; of the gift of undying life; of the deep meaning of the expression "child of God"; of faith in the Saviour.

Malan's simple words penetrated the deepest part of her being: "If you believe in Jesus, I say to you, as He said to the penitent who washed His feet with her tears, 'Go in peace; thy sins *are forgiven* thee.'" Later in her room, Elisabeth responded to the work of the Holy Spirit within her:

For the first time I seemed to forget and lose myself altogether, my struggles, my suf- ferings, my good or evil works, and could only fall on my knees in an agony of tears ... and say, "My God! guide me." I felt I was speaking to God, and that He heard me....

... I began to see that the work of our Redemption is not ours but God's, that Christ has borne away our sins, has redeemed us with His precious blood, has reconciled us to God.... The Spirit bore witness with my spirit that I was His child. I loved Him because He had first loved me! For hours I was conscious of nothing but the absorbing joy. "My Father! I am Thy child."

... [I] could seek, instead of flying from, His presence. All things were restored to harmony because [they were] restored to their true Centre.

> God loves us, not because we are worthy; but His love will make its object worthy.
> ~ César Malan
>
> H. A. César Malan, of Geneva, Switzerland, also shared the gospel with hymn-writer Charlotte Elliot, who wrote "Just As I Am."

Before, Elisabeth had been "toiling to build a tower," but her efforts had become her "pris- ons." From her conversion onward, she had no wish but that her life "might be spent in the service of Him Who had earned [her] deliv- erance at such a price- less cost. Joyful would be every toil and sacri- fice as the free service of love." She exclaimed, "From a weary labour- er, worn with slavish and ineffectual toil, I had become as a little child receiving from God."

After such a dynamic and life-changing conversion, she realized that "to follow Him Whose presence is our life and joy naturally leads us where He went and goes still, among the sorrowful and sick and perplexed." In fact, she "lived more amongst the poor than before that joy came." Her life became one characterized as not merely serving her Lord, as if to a distant Master, but as being and working in union with Him—a spontaneous, outward response to faithfully serve her indwelling Lord Jesus.

Come and Rejoice with Me!

It was after this new birth from spiritual poverty and weariness of religious service without God to untold wealth in Christ that Elisabeth wrote the poem "Come and Rejoice with Me," which she entitled "Eureka," mean-

An unveiling came to me,

NOT OF AN IDEAL, OR A THOUGHT, BUT, AS NEVER BEFORE ... A LIVING PER-SONALITY [GOD], WHICH POSSESSED MY WHOLE BEING AND CHANGED THE CURRENT OF MY THOUGHTS AND LIFE.

— ERC

ing *"I have found Him!"* How wonderful and glorious was her discovery of Christ, not through religious work, but through simple faith and obedience to Him.

But communicating this crucial difference in her relationship with God to others was not easy. It was a difficulty, Elisabeth says, "of making people who saw the new radiance with which everything shone for me understand what it was. 'You knew all this before,' they would say. And, of course, I *did* know it before; and did *not*." Knowing Jesus brought a longing "that others, also, should cross this invisible

Come and Rejoice with Me!

line between knowing about God, knowing about truth," to "knowing Him."

"NOT SUBMISSION MERELY, BUT ENTIRE ACQUIESCENCE"

At the age of twenty-three, Elisabeth married Andrew Paton Charles, a man "whose place, so quietly filled, no one else could take." Their new home in Hampstead was happily situated near some old parish almshouses where Elisabeth "had the poor, sick, and aged close" to her as she was used to before. With no children of their own to fill their lives, they instead focused on working "among the poor around the factory" where Andrew was part owner. Elisabeth also continued her writing, publishing some nineteen books during her married life.

Not long into their marriage, Andrew began having serious health problems from which he never fully recovered. After only seventeen years of companionship and service together, Andrew died, leaving Elisabeth a widow at the age of forty. Thus, she entered the darkest days of her life, which she called "that great sorrow." No longer unscathed by human suffering,

Come and Rejoice with Me!

Elisabeth does not ask for our pity in the midst of her greatest trial. For in that very year, she boldly republished her "Eureka," which she significantly retitled "Joy in Christ."

As Andrew had always embodied "the will of God, not submission merely, but entire acquiescence," Elisabeth earnestly desired to follow his example. Soon her friends began to draw her back into life by requesting translations of Martin Luther's writings and reacquainting her with the love of music. She gradually "awoke to the joys of thought, imagination and writing. The suffering grew into song and parable and story." Elisabeth soon became distinguished as one of England's best-known authors.

Although she was left without an inheritance from either her father or her husband, she was able to care for her beloved mother and many others with income from her book royalties, which she felt were "like manna from heaven." And like hidden manna, her life, her experience of Christ, her writings, and this poem will continue to feed God's seekers for generations.

From the crest of the hill overlooking the now sleeping river that stretched out from Morwellham across the English countryside toward the sea, Elisabeth reminded herself of the most important invitation she had ever received and the greatest discovery she had ever made—the one that completely changed the rest of her life.

How different was her inner condition before discovering Christ as her all-sufficient and all-supplying One! Childhood's pleasantness, even her parents, could not save her; good religious works, however well intended, had left her the more miserable and disillusioned. Thus, she had invited the One into her heart Who could make her life meaningful. Moreover, she continually came back to the One Who had brought her "from afar" to find in Him her "home." He had become her river of water of life, still flowing, supplying her every need. He had become her "treasury of love, a boundless store," from Whom she freely and ever more deeply drew deposits throughout her life. It is this secret of Christ's sufficiency she shares with all of us who heed her invitation: "Come and rejoice with me!"

If, at any time, this life of ours grows feeble, or low, or lonely, I know no other remedy than to return to its Eternal Source, to God Himself.

Lord Jesus,

Thank You for inviting me to receive You! Please come into my life right now. Free me from my striving, my efforts that change nothing, my attempts to reach Your standard, which never work. I, in this self of mine, simply cannot make it! But You died for me to meet my every need. As my doctor, heal me. As my friend, comfort me. As my mighty arm, hold me. Lift me off my feet and bring me home to Yourself. I accept Your invitation. Yes, Lord, be my joy, my sufficiency. Thank You, Lord Jesus; in You, I now rejoice!

Amen!

Come and Rejoice with Me!

Elisabeth Rundle Charles

1828–1896

Elisabeth Rundle Charles was a poet, author, linguist, musician, and painter, who became one of the best-known women in England during the nineteenth century. She was born in Tavistock, Devonshire, January 2, 1828, to Joana and John Rundle, who was a banker, businessman, and member of Parliament. He was her true friend and guide, and her mother was her devoted, life-long companion. Although not blessed with siblings, her childhood was filled with the delights of a loving extended family.

Elisabeth was educated at home in the classic disciplines and was writing poetry by age thirteen. Near age eighteen, she was led to the Lord, and from the overflowing joy of her conversion, wrote the hymn entitled "Come and Rejoice with Me!"

She was especially well known for her many books, publishing her first— a translation from the German pietist Joachim Neander—at age twenty-two. In 1863, her *Chronicles of the Schoenberg-Cotta Family*—a historical novel about the childhood of Martin Luther—became the best known of her fifty books.

At age twenty-three, she married Andrew Paton Charles, a lawyer and businessman. They were known for their philanthropic work among the poor of Wapping and Hampstead, including founding a home for incurables in 1885.

Andrew died seventeen years after their marriage, but by abundance of grace from God—Who both inspired her to write pervasively popular books of Christian history and literature and blessed her with a flow of royalties—she was able to care for her loving mother and others for many years. Elisabeth died when she was sixty-eight at Hampstead Heath, near London, March 28, 1896.

Come and Rejoice with Me!

Our Source

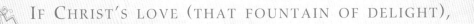 If Christ's love (that fountain of delight),

were laid as open to me as

I would wish, how I would drink,

and drink abundantly!

Samuel Rutherford

O Christ, He Is the Fountain

ANNE ROSS COUSIN

1824–1906

CHRIST IS OUR SOURCE

The water that I shall give him will become in him
a fountain of water springing up into everlasting life. (John 4:14b)

Where can we find a cool, refreshing drink of water to quench the dry, parching thirst that comes from roaming the dirty roads of this world? Can an eternal source of satisfaction for our longings be found anywhere? Yes, in fact, such a fountain freely flows in Christ Himself to all who would drink Him! When we drink Him as the living stream, we receive a refreshing supply that cannot compare to any earthly enjoyment.

Every positive attribute we need for the Christian life has its source in God and cannot naturally issue from ourselves. But we can rejoice! For He has willingly extended His mercy—expanding even "to an ocean fulness"—and we find His grace is all-sufficient. As we drink that water of life, we are satisfied and enabled to live Christ, thus expressing the divine attributes of God Himself.

In this poem, Anne Ross Cousin portrays the deep significance of the sacrifice of the Lamb of God. Jesus is the One with "piercéd hands" Who has purchased us with His precious blood—all to bring each of us as a "poor vile sinner" into "His house of wine!" What a transformation has been wrought in us and for us. The vile sinner has become His Bride! Now we "stand upon His merit," are "hidden in His presence," and are "held by His own hand." As His Bride, we delight in gazing on our dear Bridegroom's face. He has become our King of grace for eternity.

O Christ, He Is the Fountain

O Christ, He Is the Fountain

Verse One

O Christ, He is the fountain,
The deep, sweet well of life:
Its living streams I've tasted
Which save from grief and strife.
And to an ocean fulness,
His mercy doth expand;
His grace is all-sufficient
As by His wisdom planned.

Verse Two

O I am my Beloved's,
And my Beloved's mine;
He brings a poor vile sinner
Into His house of wine!
I stand upon His merit;
I know no other stand.
I'm hidden in His presence
And held by His own hand.

Verse Three

The Bride eyes not her garment,
But her dear Bridegroom's face;
I will not gaze at glory,
But on my King of grace:
Not at the crown He giveth,
But on His piercéd hand;
The Lamb is all the glory,
And my eternal stand!

Our Source

O CHRIST,
HE IS THE FOUNTAIN

Christ Is Our Source

UNTIL DEATH

The Scottish Covenanters signed the National Covenant in February 1638 to uphold the teachings and practices of the Reformation. Why would some be so impassioned to sign the covenant even with their own blood, adding "until death" to their signatures? Why would they refuse to recant and consequently suffer persecutions—including the cruelest maiming, forehead branding, torture, lifelong imprisonment, and even martyrdom?

Leading up to the National Covenant, Charles I, the king of England and Scotland, instituted severe dictates forcing the people of Scotland to strictly comply with the Prayer Book, rituals, and ecclesiastical system of the Church of England. The king conspired to gain control by requiring all ministers to implement these dictates and by replacing the noncompliant shepherds with his loyal appointees. Underlying this conflict were England's political ambitions for control over the Scottish people and their government. But for these faithful Scottish Covenanters, it was not just a political battle. They were resisting what they were convinced was apostasy in order to maintain the hard-won advances of the Reformation. Anne Ross Cousin was deeply affected by her study of these overcoming believers, but she was particularly moved by Samuel Rutherford's letters, from which she composed this hymn.

The year was 1661. Samuel Rutherford, a Scottish Covenanter, lay on his deathbed when a summons came from Edinburgh: He was commanded to appear before the next Parliament to stand trial for high treason against the newly restored monarchy of King Charles II. The charge was Rutherford's disputing the divine right of kings, as maintained in his book *Lex Rex: The Law, the King.* Because of its arguments for freedom, *Lex Rex* was found intolerable and burned, first by the hangman in Edinburgh, and later under the very windows of its author's college in St. Andrews, Scotland.

If Rutherford would not give a bold recantation of his position, he would be executed.

Unable to travel, Rutherford calmly sent a reply "that he had got another summons before a superior Judge and judicatory;" saying, "I behoove to answer my first summons; and, ere your day arrive, I will be where few kings and great folks come." Upon hearing that Rutherford was dying, Parliament voted to expel him so "that he should not be allowed to die in the college." One lawmaker, Lord Burleigh, retorted, "Ye have voted that honest man out of his college, but ye cannot vote him out of heaven."

O Christ, He Is the Fountain

SALVATION IN A LOOK

Samuel Rutherford's letters reveal a Christ Whose worth is beyond words: "But oh, He is more than my narrow praises! O time, time, flee swiftly, that our communion with Jesus may be perfected!" Almost two centuries later, Anne Ross Cousin penned her original poem of nineteen verses, weaving together selected phrases from thirty-six of Rutherford's letters.

Since Rutherford's letters became the inspiration for this exquisite hymn "O Christ, He Is the Fountain," the story behind it is also his.

Samuel Rutherford is known both for his courageous struggle to maintain scriptural truths recovered during the Reformation in Scotland and for his descriptions of the beauties of a Christ-filled life. In 1600, Rutherford was born to a respectable farming family in Nisbet Parish, Scotland. At age seventeen, he entered the college at Edinburgh, where "his talents and his industry ... carried him to the top of his classes, and all his days he could write in Latin better than either in Scotch or English." Due to his academic success,

Time Standeth Not Still

RUTHERFORD'S EXHORTATION
TO A LANDOWNER:

SIR, THERE IS A GREAT DEAL LESS SAND IN YOUR GLASS THAN WHEN I SAW YOU.... YE EAT AND DRINK, BUT TIME STANDETH NOT STILL; YE LAUGH, BUT YOUR DAY FLEETH AWAY.... LAY YOUR SOUL AND YOUR WEIGHTS UPON GOD. MAKE HIM YOUR ONLY, ONLY BEST-BELOVED.

SR

O Christ, He Is the Fountain

Rutherford was appointed Professor of Humanity at the young age of twenty-three. Around the same time, he was converted to Christ, later confessing, "Oh but Christ hath a saving eye! ... When He first looked on me, I was saved; it cost Him but a look to make hell quit of me!" It was love at first sight, and Rutherford's life was forever changed.

HIS MERCY DOTH EXPAND

Rutherford went on to complete his studies in theology, and thereafter was appointed to the tiny backwoods hamlet called Anwoth, where he shepherded the flock "scattered over a hilly district" for nine years:

See him passing along yonder field and climbing that hill on his way to some cottage.... He has time to visit, for he rises at three in the morning, and at that early hour meets his God in prayer and meditation, and has space for study besides.... Men said of him, "He is always praying, always preaching, always visiting the sick, always catechizing, always writing and studying." He was known to fall asleep at night talking of Christ and even to speak of Him during his sleep. Indeed, he himself speaks of his dreams being of Christ.

Each Christian in Anwoth Parish was the object of Rutherford's care, but "over the unsaved he yearned most tenderly." He implored, "Oh, if ye would fall in love with Him, how blessed were I! How glad would my soul be to help you to love Him!" Rutherford longed to help each soul drink from the deep, sweet well of the Savior. "Christ, nothing but Christ, can cool our love's burning languor." He prayed earnestly to be able to distribute "the great Loaf, Christ, to the children of His family."

Rutherford further spoke to his flock of the deepening relationship of Christ with His beloved Bride. He desired that each "poor vile sinner" would be brought into the Lord's "house of wine." He told them, "Know, therefore, ... our Lord Jesus cometh to woo a bride."

Christ as "All Things"

BLESSED WERE WE IF WE COULD MAKE
OURSELVES MASTER OF THAT INVALU-
ABLE TREASURE, THE LOVE OF CHRIST;
OR RATHER SUFFER OURSELVES TO BE
MASTERED AND SUBDUED TO CHRIST'S
LOVE SO AS CHRIST WERE OUR "ALL
THINGS," AND ALL OTHER THINGS OUR
NOTHINGS.

SR

He exhorted, "Be content ... every day to be adding ... to your wedding garment, that ye may be at last decored and trimmed as a bride for Christ, ... beautified in the hidden man of the heart."

Rutherford's joy at shepherding in Anwoth was mingled with suffering, including the deaths of his two children in infancy. Additionally, before his wife's death, she suffered from a yearlong illness so intense that Rutherford described her as in "great torment and pain night and day.... She sleeps none, and cries as a woman travailing in birth." In the midst of this, Rutherford also endured an incapacitating fever for more than three months. Of these sufferings, Rutherford proclaimed, "Welcome, welcome, cross of Christ, if Christ be with it. An afflicted life looks very like the way that leads to the kingdom."

BY HIS WISDOM PLANNED

In 1636, Rutherford published a treatise in defense of grace that revealed his nonconformity to the religious authorities of the time. For this stance, the High Court removed him from Anwoth and sent him to Aberdeen to suffer town arrest. Furthermore, he was forbidden to preach in the pulpit: "Next to Christ, I had but one joy, the apple of the eye of my delights, to preach Christ, my Lord; and they have violently plucked that away from me." He mourned, "My dumb Sabbaths burden my heart and make it bleed." "The banished minister," as he was known in the town, was openly shunned on the streets—the authorities giving him the coldest reception of all. Yet, many townspeople secretly sought his counsel. He admitted,

"I find folks here kind to me, but in the night and under their breath." He continued to share Christ with his frequent visitors, which further angered town authorities.

While he suffered thus outwardly, Rutherford realized the true source of grief and strife resides within man. He wrote, "Oh, that I were free of that idol which they call myself.... Oh, but we have much need to be ransomed and redeemed by Christ from that master-tyrant, that cruel and lawless lord, *ourself*."

Furthermore, he exposed the foolish and false enticements that the world feeds upon:

Draw by the lap of time's curtain, ... look in ... to great and endless eternity, and consider if a worldly price (suppose this little round clay globe of this ashy and dirty earth, the dining idol of the fools of this world, were all your own) can be given for one smile of Christ's Godlike and soul-ravishing countenance.

O Christ, He Is the Fountain

Though deeply afflicted by separation from his flock, Rutherford submitted to God's sovereign arrangement. In fact, these trials yielded a fragrance of resurrection wafting from the hundreds of letters he wrote to his loved ones back home: "His fair face, His lovely and kindly kisses, have made me, a poor prisoner, see that there is more to be had of Christ in this life than I believed! ... But yet I know it is more: it is the kingdom of God within us." His correspondents began sharing his exhorting and encouraging letters with one another, leading to a compilation in book form that preserved Rutherford's letters through the centuries as a lasting memorial of the loveliness of Christ, Who was his "King of grace."

My Sadness for His Joys, My Losses for His Presence

Due to the imposition of Anglican liturgy in worship, a Scottish uprising occurred that culminated in the signing of the National Covenant in 1638. Because of this political and religious turn of events, Rutherford was given back the care of his beloved flock in Anwoth. However, his godly influence was needed at St. Andrews, the oldest university in Scotland. Though saddened to leave Anwoth just a year after returning, he accepted his appointment as professor with the stipulation that he should not be subjected to another "dumb Sabbath." Thus, he was able to preach his beloved Christ in local parishes every weekend, in addition to fervently laboring at the university for more than twenty years. He influenced many college students, who were known for their profane conversation and error in doctrine.

Rutherford was sent as one of four Scottish representatives to the historic Westminster Assembly in London, where they labored to define and

O Christ, He Is the Fountain

uphold the fundamental beliefs and practices of the Reformation in Britain. During those four years away from the college, he endured ill health and suffered the loss of six children from his second marriage. Nevertheless, he affirmed, "My Lord Jesus hath fully recompensed my sadness with His joys, my losses with His own presence."

In 1661, the tides of government changed yet again, and Charles II was crowned. Many of the Scottish Covenanters became martyrs under the ensuing wave of persecution. Rutherford was no exception. Even then it was said of him, "His talents, his industry, his scholarship, his preaching power, his pastoral solicitude and his saintly character all combined to make Rutherford a marked man both to the friends and to the enemies of the truth." But before the next Parliament could pronounce a judgment of death for his position in *Lex Rex*, Samuel Rutherford was beholding the face of the Lord Jesus in righteousness. He, like the psalmist in the midst of his enemies, was satisfied to awake in His likeness.

Throughout his yielded life, Rutherford had proclaimed of the Lord, "He Himself visiteth my soul with feasts of spiritual comforts. Oh, how sweet a Master is Christ!" Rutherford had learned contentment in Christ. No gathering storm clouds could diminish his inner joy, his enjoyment of "that deep, sweet well of life." In a letter, he asserted:

> *The serving of the world and sin hath but a base reward and smoke instead of pleasures.... Go where you will, your soul shall not sleep soundly but in Christ's bosom.*

Rutherford received his sufferings without bitterness. He viewed his trials as opportunities to discover more divine treasures. Rutherford urged,

> *Be humbled; walk softly. Down, down, for God's sake.... Stoop, stoop! it is a low entry to go in.... Come in, come in to Christ, and see what ye want, and find it in Him.*

O Christ, He Is the Fountain

"O Christ, He Is the Fountain" expresses God's plan for the glorious relationship between Christ and His corporate Bride for eternity. Because of Christ's great love and longing for His Bride, He is perfecting her to be His loving counterpart. Samuel Rutherford yearned earnestly for his Beloved's return and "the dawning of the marriage-day!" With sweet anticipation, he exclaimed, "Oh, if He would fold the heavens together like an old cloak, and shovel time and days out of the way, and make ready in haste the Lamb's Wife for her Husband!" All through his lifetime, he gave the Lamb all the glory, for he had only one prayerful desire:

God send me no more,
for my part of paradise, but Christ.

Lord Jesus,

Your hands were pierced for me, a poor vile sinner, and You have become a deep, sweet well of life to save me! Now, I am hidden in Your presence, and I stand upon Your merit. You are my Most Beloved One, Bridegroom, and King of grace. I love You. Glory! Glory! The Lamb is all the Glory!

Amen!

Anne Ross Cousin

1824–1906

Born in Kingston-upon-Hull, England, in 1824, Anne Ross Cundell Cousin was the only daughter of Dr. David Ross Cundell of Leith, a surgeon who served with the Thirty-third Regiment in the British army at the Battle of Waterloo. When Anne was three years old, her father died, and her mother moved with Anne to Edinburgh, Scotland.

In 1847, Anne married William Cousin, a Scotsman from Leith, who was a minister in Chelsea, London. They later served in Irvine, Aryshire, and Melrose, Roxburghshire, Scotland, where they had one son, John, and two daughters, Anne and Isabella.

Around the year 1856 while in Irvine, Mrs. Cousin read the letters of Scottish Covenanter Samuel Rutherford, a native of Roxburghshire, who struggled to maintain the progress of the Reformation two centuries earlier. As she reflected upon his letters while sewing, she weaved lines of poetry together, ultimately using expressions from thirty-six of his letters and his final words to create a poetic tapestry of nineteen verses titled "The Sands of Time Are Sinking." This work was later condensed into a hymn called "Immanuel's Land" or "Rutherford's Hymn" and published in *The Christian Treasury* in 1857.

Anne Ross Cousin composed many more poems and hymns, publishing 107 in all. Her other best-loved hymn is "O Christ, What Burdens Bow'd Thy Head." She also wrote *Memorials of Scottish Martyrs and Confessors of the Seventeenth Century* and *The Last Words of Rev. Samuel Rutherford: With Some of His Sweet Sayings.* She died on December 6, 1906, in Edinburgh at the age of eighty-two.

O Christ, He Is the Fountain

Our Supply

 As the deer pants

for the water brooks,

so pants my soul for You,

O God. *Psalms 42:1*

I Cannot Breathe Enough of Thee

WILLIAM SPENCER WALTON

1850–1906

CHRIST IS OUR SUPPLY

My beloved spoke, and said to me:
"Rise up, my love, my fair one, and come away." ... My beloved is mine,
and I am his. (Song of Songs 2:10, 16)

Captivated by the Lord's beauty, William Spencer Walton could describe only by metaphor that intrinsic ecstasy he shared with his Lord. He experienced God as a fragrant "gentle breeze of love," the "Fairest of the Fair," and the One with "the sweetest name on earth," Whose whisper assures "All is well."

No mere composition of flowery words, this hymn is weighty in the experiential aspects of divine romance: God's heart of love is fixed on us, and we return His love as His redeemed eternal companions. We are espoused to Him and will forever be His Bride!

What a mystery that we could so intensely love One Whom we have never seen with physical eyes! Yet as our hearts turn to the Lord, He removes the veil and we see our Beloved, Who is the "Fairest of the Fair." To gain an intimate relationship with the Lord Jesus is our greatest opportunity while here on earth—for we who enter into it are forever changed. As we behold His "face of radiancy," divine glory shines into our hearts, and our love for Him flows spontaneously and irresistibly. When our ordinary and mundane lives are filled and brightened with Him, we will declare with William Spencer Walton:

I cannot breathe enough of Thee,
I cannot gaze enough on Thee,
I cannot yield enough to Thee,
I cannot sing enough of Thee,
I cannot speak enough of Thee.

I Cannot Breathe Enough of Thee

I Cannot Breathe Enough of Thee

Verse One

I cannot breathe enough of Thee,
O gentle breeze of love;
More fragrant than the myrtle tree
The Henna-flower is to me,
    The Balm of Heaven above,
    The Balm of Heaven above.

Verse Two

I cannot gaze enough on Thee,
Thou Fairest of the Fair;
My heart is filled with ecstasy,
As in Thy face of radiancy
    I see such beauty there,
    I see such beauty there.

Verse Three

I cannot yield enough to Thee,
My Savior, Master, Friend;
I do not wish to go out free,
But ever, always, willingly,
    To serve Thee to the end,
    To serve Thee to the end.

Verse Four

I cannot sing enough of Thee,
The sweetest name on earth;
A note so full of melody
Comes from my heart so joyously,
    And fills my soul with mirth,
    And fills my soul with mirth.

Verse Five

I cannot speak enough of Thee,
I have so much to tell;
Thy heart it beats so tenderly
As Thou dost draw me close to Thee,
    And whisper, "All is well,"
    And whisper, "All is well."

Our Supply

I Cannot Breathe
Enough of Thee

Christ Is Our Supply

CONTINENT IN CHAOS

By the conclusion of the nineteenth century, the continent of Africa had been suffering not only from the social unrest leading up to the Boer War, but also from one physical calamity after another. Extended drought plunged Africa into famine, which weakened the population's general health and impoverished farmers. Locusts ravaged food crops, and malnourishment intensified devastating diseases. Starvation and death were rampant, and native tribes were decimated. Moreover, a virulent plague reduced cattle herds by more than 90 percent. As a result, abandoned rangeland became the breeding ground for a tsetse fly infestation that transmitted parasites and disease from wild animals to domestic animals and humans, killing nearly two hundred thousand people from 1902 to 1906. These withering sufferings opened the doors for evangelists to bring the good news of Jesus Christ to the once-closed continent. In 1888, the Lord called William Spencer Walton into Africa.

In the 1840s, in the Scottish Highlands, a seed of divine intention for Africa was germinated:

A solitary shepherd was tending his flock, alone to the outward eye, but on that lonely moor he knew the sweet companionship of his Lord. The sun was setting, and the air was filled with the fragrance of the sweet heather. On his knees, his head buried in his plaid, the shepherd was pleading with his God. It was no unusual experience with that old Highlander. Many a time the hush had been broken by the strong cries and prayers of that servant of God. He was pleading for God's blessing on Africa's unevangelized millions.... In that dark mine of sin he knew there were precious gems to be found for the Master's crown.

A half century later, William Spencer Walton earnestly pondered a map of Africa while aboard a steamer ship on his homeward voyage from that continent. His eyes fixed on Swaziland, and he exclaimed, "Swaziland for Christ!" He could not know then how instrumental he would be in bringing the gospel to this land—a direct answer to the old Highlander's prayers. These were threads woven together by God's sovereign hand.

BREATHING IN THE GENTLE BREEZE

Walton's hymn "I Cannot Breathe Enough of Thee" reveals the extent to which he was quietly content and at rest in Christ while so active in service. His Christian journey began with a dynamic conversion and subsequent immersion into evangelistic activity. Yet, as he breathed the Lord as a "gentle breeze of love," he learned to maintain his fellowship with the indwelling Lord.

William Spencer Walton was born in London on January 15, 1850. His mother, Martha, was "a woman of beautiful disposition and saintly character, and her influence over Spencer was always very great." As a youth, Spencer was known for "a love of fun and mischief, which marked him out as leader in many an escapade." As a young adult, though he appeared religious on Sundays, he had yet to meet the Savior. He felt that before he received the Lord Jesus, he was a profligate hypocrite—present to teach Sunday school after having partied till the wee hours of dawn.

The first great sorrow in Walton's life occurred when he was only fifteen. He was on a lengthy voyage, necessitated by his poor health, when his forty-year-old father died. The news was more difficult to bear because it reached him long afterward in distant Australia. Far from his cheerful home, he was all alone, ill, and now fatherless.

In 1872, a series of events further softened Walton's heart toward Christ. He was confronted with his own mortality when he learned that a close friend had suddenly died from blood poisoning. While the "solemnizing effect" was still upon him, Walton further learned of his "true condition" through a pivotal word from a mission preacher. Later, Walton's younger brother invited him to hear an evangelist. Afterward, Walton straightforwardly asked him, "Sir, how do I get to God?" The evangelist led him to the Savior. Walton began associating with the British Plymouth Brethren, whereupon he fell in love with the Bible. At times, he greeted the dawn still reading the Word of God.

SOMETHING DIVINELY COMPREHENSIBLE

Infilled with the Divine Life, Walton sought to channel God's overflowing love through gospel service. He and his friends began to host evening open-air gospel meetings. However, his first message was cut short when a listener spit in his face. Feeling that he had failed God, "that night, upon his knees, he definitely claimed from God power for service, and as definitely pleaded that the gift of the evangelist might be his."

Through 1882, Walton continued his gospel labor while working full-time, though he "pined for the day when the fetters of business should be broken." One of his coworkers observed that Walton was "a man so beautiful in his simpleness of purpose, his consecration to God," that he further affirmed, "I at once longed for a like experience of the Divine Life within, affecting, transforming the whole being, and shedding gracious influence on those around."

Later that year, Walton relinquished his business and joined a missionary society that took him throughout the British Isles. His labor was marked by two life practices: "his intense love for the Word of God, and his unceasing habit of prayer." On the last day of 1884, Walton was driven to "a real time of prayer," wherein he left the missionary society. His reason was "not to confine himself to one branch of Christ's Church, but to take up general and undenominational mission work." Learning to depend entirely on the Lord, he wrote, "I do not want to see the future, but the Lord will ... provide.... Oh it is such perfect rest."

Walton realized that he was "not merely set apart for work ... but set apart for Himself." This theme would govern the remainder of his Christian life:

There is a stillness in the Christian's life: ...
But known to those who in this stillness rest,
Something divinely comprehensible.
That for my nothingness I GET GOD'S BEST.

GRACE ABOUNDING; AFRICA CALLING

Walton continued mission work at home, but the "more urgent claims of the lands where as yet Christ was unknown" were beckoning. The Lord began clarifying His master plan for Walton. At the Keswick Convention of 1882, he met Andrew Murray, who was laboring for the

Lord in South Africa. Murray indicated that if Walton were led there, he would be the first to welcome him "in the name of the Lord." Additionally, another missionary at the convention "prayed to be guided aright" before compelling him to consider South Africa. Walton sought further fellowship with others such as Hudson Taylor and F. B. Meyer. A final confirmation came to Walton in these words from a devotional book: "Make me such a faithful steward as not to go an inch from Thy will, but on all occasions to act and suffer according to Thy pleasure." Hence, Walton accepted God's clear calling to South Africa.

Within a month of his arrival, more than five hundred people "professed conversion," many of whom became future laborers for Christ.

From 1888 until 1904, Walton labored tirelessly with Andrew Murray and others, enjoying the Lord's abundant blessing. Walton recalls a tribal king in Tongaland who, after being taught to read the Bible, told the missionaries that "he was more hungry for Jesus than for his daily food, and was eager to follow Him." Overall, the regular work at the outposts was characterized as "quiet, solid, and ever-extending."

SWEET SUPPLIES

In 1889, Walton married Kathleen Mary Dixon, who happily entered into his labors in South Africa. In ten months, they were blessed with the birth of a son. Tragically, two weeks later Kathleen passed away, leaving behind "the blessed influence of her fragrant life." Looking to Christ for comfort, Walton found Him as his "Savior, Master, Friend." Determined to know the Lord ever more deeply in mourning, he wrote:

I cannot always trace His ways
Through cloud, through storm, through calm,
But this I know; if He should wound,
I always have His balm.

After years of enduring more hardships in South Africa, Walton described the Lord's faithful care:

He has been our Guide, our Way, our Protector, our Provision, He has been our All in every step of the way.... We have drawn from Him sweet supplies, enough to spare.

Walton was ever more focused on experiencing Christ, writing, "We know Him and that is more than enough." Later, the Lord graced Walton in marriage to Miss Lena Gibson.

I Cannot Breathe Enough of Thee

Together, they continued the mission work in South Africa.

As Walton crossed the great rivers in Africa and witnessed Niagara Falls in America, he compared their strength and beauty to the fountain of the Lord's life within him:

The falls ... baffle description.... But what appealed to me were the possibilities of all this mighty power. "Out of him shall flow rivers of living water" was continually suggested to me. Out of me, out of God's weakest child, a mightier power than Niagara can flow.... Oh, to be in His hands, quiet, trustful, surrendered that His power may flow through me.

THY WILL: NOTHING ELSE

After the Boer War broke out in 1899, Walton ministered food, medicine, and grace to missionaries escaping from the interior of Swaziland and to thousands of refugees pouring into Durban. In spite of the danger, Walton felt called to the front lines throughout the war.

Once, even as he stepped off the train, a stream of soldiers gladly received more than six hundred copies of the New Testament. Oftentimes, Walton and others ministered in the army hospitals and on the campgrounds:

Every evening, on the veldt between the lines, with no canopy but the purple African sky, we held a service, the congregation numbering three, four, or five hundred. By the light of hurricane lanterns ... hymns were sung, the men lying prone ... or standing in groups.... All seemed softened and rendered impressionable ... by the sickness and death so prevalent around.

After the war, Walton prospected for new mission stations. The compassion of God welled up within him upon sighting Kosi Bay, and his plea echoed the old Scottish Highlander's prayer of many decades earlier:

This is an untouched *district with a people lying in darkness, and in the shadow of death,* without a single witness *to carry to them the Gospel of Christ.... God forbid that we should be slack to go in and possess this land for Him. Never before in South Africa have I seen such an open door, where the people are asking for missionaries and willing to receive them.*

By 1904, the handful of laborers with whom Walton had arrived in South Africa had become an army of more than one hundred

ENTRY IN WALTON'S DIARY
JUST PRIOR TO THE BOER WAR:

JANUARY 15, 1899.
RESOLVED IN HIS STRENGTH:–
— TO BE MORE CAREFUL IN
    MY EXPENDITURE.
— TO HAVE MORE TIME ALONE
    WITH GOD.
— TO BE MORE CAREFUL AND PRAYER-
    FUL IN MY STUDY OF GOD'S WORD.
— TO ASK HIM MORE ABOUT
    LITTLE THINGS.
O LORD! WHAT WILT THOU
HAVE ME TO DO?

W. SPENCER WALTON,
A BONDSERVANT OF JESUS CHRIST

workers stationed at far-reaching outposts. That same year, the Walton family sailed from South Africa to travel abroad on behalf of the mission. As they left behind their beloved Africa, they had ample "assurance ... that He Who had led would lead" in their absence and in their future.

On August 22, 1906, in the midst of their travels, Walton developed a life-threatening abdominal infection. Four days later, Mrs. Walton felt she must tell him he would soon die. From the rich depths of abiding in Christ, he responded, *"He knows! I'm ready. I've been ready for thirty-four years. Bless His Name!"*

Walton breached the veil of time and place on August 26, 1906.

Walton declared that his entire Christian life had been "grace upon grace all along; mercy from first to last." These are the opening words of his diary the year he passed away:

The fulness of the riches of God in Christ Jesus—all mine. Praise the Lord! Thy will:—nothing more, nothing less, nothing else.

Lord Jesus,

You are my gentle, fragrant breeze of love to refresh my heart. You are the sweetest name on earth that makes my heart sing joyously. And You are the tender heart that draws me close to You, whispering, "All is well." Help make this experience my daily reality. I love You, Lord!

Amen

William Spencer Walton
1850–1906

William Spencer Walton was born in London, England, on January 15, 1850, to Charles and Martha Walton. He enjoyed a pleasant childhood despite being physically frail. However, his security was shattered at age fifteen by the early death of his father.

From his salvation at age twenty-two, Walton immersed himself in the Word of God and prayed for the gift of evangelism. He served the Lord in business and evening evangelism until 1882, at which time he joined a mission society and labored in the British Isles until he was called to South Africa. During his first trip in 1888, hundreds were led to Christ. Walton then returned to England to establish the Cape General Mission in 1889.

While in England, he married Kathleen Mary Dixon, and they traveled to South Africa to serve together. Sadly, after only ten months together, Kathleen died soon after their son was born. Walton continued to labor in South Africa, learning deeper trust in his indwelling Lord.

In 1893, Walton married Lena Gibson, and they served the Lord in South Africa through intense personal loss, war, famine, and plagues. In 1894, the Cape General Mission merged with another mission to become the South Africa General Mission, formed for the purpose of evangelizing and shepherding the indigenous and Europeans alike. Walton became its first director.

In 1904, the Waltons, with their three children, were sent to minister in North America and Britain for the mission. Walton continued serving and enjoying Christ as his true supply until his death on August 26, 1906, at the age of fifty-six.

I Cannot Breathe Enough of Thee

His Availability

 HE BREAKS THE POWER OF CANCELLED SIN,

HE SETS THE PRISONER FREE;

HIS BLOOD CAN MAKE THE FOULEST CLEAN;

HIS BLOOD AVAILED FOR ME.

Charles Wesley

And Can It Be?

CHARLES WESLEY
1707–1788

His Availability

In the beginning was the Word, and the Word was with God, and the Word was God.
And the Word became flesh and dwelt among us. (John 1:1, 14a)

Could God, Who is ever-existing and indestructible, die? Is He not the same One Who in the beginning framed the worlds by the Word of His mouth? Charles Wesley stood in awe of the eternal, mighty God becoming a fragile creature; clothing Himself in flesh and blood to be incarnated as a man—the man Christ Jesus. Why? To be crucified! To redeem the very ones who had put Him to death! The mystery of His death is of universal proportions.

The beginning word of this hymn, "and," speaks of Wesley's amazement that he himself received a beneficial share in this monumental act of sacrificial love. God died for all of mankind "and" even for Wesley, whose unregenerate, rebellious, sinful self had "Him to death pursued."

The countless sins of each generation have proved how hopelessly impossible it is for man to please God. So, according to His plan, God in Christ "emptied Himself of all but love, and bled for Adam's helpless race!" Jesus' sinless life satisfied the Old Testament requirements and qualified Him to be God's unique offering for man's redemption. His all-problem-solving death blotted out every charge that condemned us.

The fate of the universe, mankind, and all creation hinged upon this marvelous redemption! Human history changed forever on that day as an entirely new covenant of grace and mercy emerged with Christ from the grave. Christ's resurrection is evidence that God accepted Him as the One qualified to pay our debt in full. In His all-grace-releasing resurrection, we became alive to God and now may joyfully affirm with Charles Wesley—

Yes, it can be!

And Can It Be?

And Can It Be?

Verse One

And can it be that I should gain
An int'rest in the Savior's blood?
Died He for me, who caused His pain?
For me, who Him to death pursued?
Amazing love! how can it be
That Thou, my God, shouldst die for me?

Verse Two

'Tis mystery all! The Immortal dies!
Who can explore His strange design?
In vain the firstborn seraph tries
To sound the depths of love Divine!
'Tis mercy all! let earth adore,
Let angel minds inquire no more.

Verse Three

He left His Father's throne above,
So free, so infinite His grace;
Emptied Himself of all but love,
And bled for Adam's helpless race:
'Tis mercy all, immense and free;
For, O my God, it found out me.

Verse Four

Long my imprisoned spirit lay
Fast bound in sin and nature's night;
Thine eye diffused a quickening ray,
I woke, the dungeon flamed with light;
My chains fell off, my heart was free,
I rose, went forth, and followed Thee.

Verse Five

No condemnation now I dread;
Jesus, and all in Him, is mine!
Alive in Him, my living Head,
And clothed in righteousness Divine,
Bold I approach the eternal throne,
And claim the crown,
   through Christ my own.

AND CAN IT BE?

IMPENDING REVOLUTION

During the eighteenth century, English society was influenced by the philosophy of the Enlightenment, with its rejection of faith and its foundational belief that unending progress could be achieved through human reasoning alone. The Wesley brothers witnessed firsthand the waste and ruin that this godless philosophy brought forth.

Revolution was coming! England was plunged into a roiling cauldron of unrest: It was embroiled with a deadly combination of impersonal state religion, an aloof and arrogant aristocracy, and the angry masses who were afflicted by industrialization's dehumanizing misery and blight. In response, God raised up men like Charles and John Wesley to issue in the Age of Faith to ensure that this revolution would be a spiritual one.

Shortly after his conversion to Christ, Charles Wesley was ministering the gospel to the men condemned to death at London's Newgate prison. In one cell, he came upon a feverish black man sentenced to death for having robbed his master. Wesley recounted,

I told him of One Who came down from heaven to save lost sinners, and him in particular; [I] described the sufferings of the Son of God, His sorrows, agony, and death. He listened with all the signs of eager astonishment; the tears trickled down his cheeks while he cried, "What? Was it for me? Did He suffer all this for so poor a creature as me?"

Wesley was deeply moved:

I found myself overwhelmed with the love of Christ to sinners.

The night before the executions, Wesley and his fellow minister Mr. Bray remained locked in with those prisoners who were condemned to die early the next morning. One by one, each prisoner's expression was transported from that of hopelessness and the dread of impending death to peacefulness and the promise of eternal life.

Morning came and with it the cart that carried the condemned men to the gallows. All the way, Wesley comforted those about to die. He led them to sing a hymn his father had written:

Behold the Saviour of mankind,
*   Nail'd to the shameful tree!*
How vast the love that Him inclined
*   To bleed and die for thee!*

'Tis done! the precious ransom's paid;
*   "Receive my soul!" He cries;*
See where He bows His sacred head!
*   He bows His head, and dies.*

And Can It Be?

Wesley continued to bestow prayers and tender love, even kisses, upon each man he could reach; then he led them in a hymn that included this verse:

A guilty, weak and helpless worm,
  Into thy hands I fall;
Be thou my life, my righteousness,
  My Jesus and my all.

The men were led to the scaffold, and a rope was slung around each neck. The whip cracked, the horses sprang forward, and the cart lurched away. As the men plunged downward, not one bristled or resisted, for they could now face God in peace.

Wesley shared a few final words of comfort to the witnessing crowd. Later, he summarized this most moving experience: "[We] returned full of peace in our friends' happiness. That hour under the gallows was the most blessed hour of my life." Such was the depth of love Wesley had for both God and man.

And Can It Be?

SPECIAL CAPACITIES SHINING FORTH

Charles Wesley was born in 1707, the eighteenth child of Samuel and Susanna Wesley, and the ninth to survive infancy, the other nine buried side by side in the family churchyard. His father was an Anglican minister, and a "lifelong and painstaking student and interpreter of the Scriptures" and of the ancient languages of "Hebrew, Chaldee, Syriac, Arabic, Greek, and Latin." The elder Wesley wrote *History of the Old and New Testaments* in three volumes of rhyme, reflecting special capacities that would shine forth in his third son.

His mother managed a well-ordered home with an emphasis on spiritual training.

Consequently, "the careful use of time, regularity for meals, family devotions morning and evening ... to all this [Charles] was accustomed, probably more than any other eight-year-old boy in England." From the age of eight to thirty, "he was so immersed in the ... great men of the bygone era" of Greece and Rome that he "took on their habits of mind and their forms of expression." After an education in the classics at Westminster Abbey, where he rose to the equivalent of student-body president, he followed his brother John to Oxford in 1726 as a "King's Scholar."

Concerning the Wesleys' time at Oxford, "these were the days in which the standards of the nation had been grievously lowered. Drunkenness, gambling, stealing and immorality were common, and Deism—the

> *And can it be that I should gain*
> *An int'rest in the Savior's blood?*
>
> Wesley saw himself as the direct cause of Christ's sufferings and death. He was not an innocent business partner—he was not even an honest competitor. He was, in fact, the Lord's sworn enemy, "who Him to death pursued!" Yet, Wesley was amazed to discover that at Christ's death, he had become a shareholder with an "interest" in Christ's redemptive work. He had been made Christ's beneficiary, the direct object of His love!

And Can It Be?

belief that God is merely an impersonal 'First Cause'—was widely accepted." Though somewhat influenced in his first year, Charles preserved his vessel: "'Tis owing, in great measure, to somebody's prayers (my mother's most likely) that ... I awoke out of my lethargy." Charles did more than shake off his own lethargy; he "persuaded two or three young scholars ... to observe the method of study prescribed by the Statutes of the University." For this, he was called a "Methodist." Shortly thereafter, the "Holy Club" was begun. At that time, Charles convinced George Whitefield, the future gospel messenger to America, to be a member. But as yet, Whitefield and the Wesleys, the unprecedented evangelistic trio, did not know for themselves true conversion to Christ.

In 1735, Charles' father, Samuel, was suffering his final bout with illness and was nigh to death. He prophetically said to Charles: "Be steady. The Christian faith will surely revive in this kingdom; you shall see it, though I shall not." Of Samuel it was said that he "was far in advance of his sons, both in evangelical knowledge and spiritual attainments. He enjoyed the Christian salvation, the nature and method of which neither John nor Charles at that time understood. When their views of divine truth were corrected and matured, they simply taught what their venerable parent experienced and testified upon the bed of death."

And Can It Be?

That same year, Charles and John went on a missionary trip to Georgia. During the voyage, an exceedingly violent storm with massive waves shattered the mainsail and penetrated the main cabin:

Most of the passengers were overcome by fear, but while they screamed in terror, the Moravians, who were in the midst of a hymn while the storm was at its worst, calmly continued to sing and pray. John asked if one of them was afraid. He answered, "I thank God, no." "But, were your women and children not afraid?" He replied mildly, "No, our women and children are not afraid to die." John admits ... he himself was filled with fear.... He knew nothing of the peace these people possessed. This was the first experience of evangelical Christianity, and it left a mark that would not be erased.

The Moravians' trust amid the storm created disquietude within the Wesleys, unveiling their deepest need for the Prince of Peace.

The missionary trip ended in disappointment. Vexed and discouraged, Charles would learn through harsh experience the failure and hopelessness of his strict methodistic practices: a lethal combination of self-manufactured piety, negative legalism, and heavy-handed church discipline. There was no life ministered because "his only message ... was one of works, and he was still unaware of the great, fundamental truth that he was soon to experience ... of 'justification by faith.'"

FROM WORKS TO GRACE

Soon after returning to England, Charles and John became "aware that there is such an experience as 'the new birth.'" Their friend

And Can It Be?

> *In vain the firstborn seraph tries*
> *To sound the depths of love Divine!*

This phrase refers to Lucifer, later called Satan, who always attempts in vain to test the depths of God's love. "To sound" is a nautical term Wesley used to describe Satan's scheme to deceive fallen mankind into believing we are beyond the depths of God's love! But while the ocean's depth is finite and measurable, God's love is limitless and unfathomable!

George Whitefield had recently received the Lord Jesus, and Charles heard him preach to seeking throngs: "Ye must be born again." Soon afterward, the Moravian Peter Bohler shared daily with Charles and John that the way to be saved was not by best endeavors, but by faith in Christ. Meanwhile, they each had been reading different writings of Martin Luther, "who set both brothers before the door of faith and put their hands on its handle."

Charles became ill and was being cared for by the Bray family. Mr. Bray prayed and read the Scriptures with him. "God sent Mr. Bray ..., a poor ignorant mechanic, who knows nothing but Christ; yet by knowing Him, knows and discerns all things." To Charles, Sunday, May 21, 1738, "was the day of deliverance, ... the day for which he will borrow the experience of Peter in the jail of Herod, or Paul in the prison at Philippi, and the language of David, Isaiah, and Jesus Christ." At last, he believed! The writing of "And Can It Be?" is closely connected to his conversion to Christ. Only days before, he had written,

> *Weary of struggling with my pain*
> *Hopeless to trust my nature's chain.*

And Can It Be?

But, as one redeemed, he marveled:

How shall I all to heaven aspire?
A slave redeemed from death and sin,
A brand pluck'd from eternal fire.

A significant load of self-imposed striving was lifted, releasing what he described as "a new enthusiasm, a new glow, a spiritual buoyancy." Charles felt this way: "I now found myself at peace with God, and rejoiced in hope." And John would trust in Christ and be saved three days later!

GRACE ABOUNDING IN THE OPEN AIR

George Whitefield, who pioneered the preaching of the gospel in the open air to literally tens of thousands, led Charles and John Wesley to join him, thus propelling them into their prevailing ministry. By being barred from the pulpit, the Wesleys were used to reach the English masses who most needed to hear the gospel. Crowds of "ten thousand helpless sinners waiting" for an invitation to Christ gathered in fields and parks. Charles spoke "of a 'supernatural strength' given to him in his preaching and of a spiritual joy so intense that both he and his hearers were overcome with tears of delight." The Wesleys eventually traveled as itinerant gospel messengers, preaching across a giant circuit in all of England.

However, eighteenth-century England's spiritual revolution was obtained at great cost. The Wesleys often suffered persecution from angry mobs who cursed, beat, and stoned them in village after village. The ruffians, under no restraint from the authorities, attacked the Wesleys with "fierceness and diabolical mal-

And Can It Be?

ice." Nevertheless, when the rabble met with the love of Christ, many repented and turned to Him. The revolution of repentance spread throughout all of England, as Charles said, "All opposition falls before us, or rather is fallen ... this also the Lord wrought."

Charles Wesley's call to evangelism could be seen throughout more than fifty years of preaching Christ. As he lay dying, he dictated lines of his final poem to his wife, expressing his eternal hope in Christ:

Jesus, my only hope Thou art,
Strength of my failing flesh and heart.

Lord Jesus,

Thank You for Your amazing love! I was Your enemy; I did not love You, but You died for me! Your precious blood avails to cleanse my every failure and sin! I was bound and chained, but Your light pierced through my chains, into my heart, and now I am alive in You! Thank You for exchanging my dread and condemnation for joy and infinite grace!

Amen

And Can It Be?

Charles Wesley

1707–1788

Charles Wesley was born on the frigid day of December 18 in 1707, eight weeks premature. His parents looked at his motionless body and thought he was stillborn. However, this eighteenth child of Samuel and Susanna Wesley survived to become a faithful servant of God. On April 8, 1749, Wesley married Sarah ("Sally") Gwynne. They had eight children, of whom only four survived infancy.

Earlier, while studying at Oxford, Charles and his brother John started the "Holy Club." In their pursuit of a holy life, the members met regularly for Bible study, fellowship, and prayer, and also to minister in the prison. All of this, though sincerely done for God, was also done without God. Later, both brothers acknowledged that, during their time at Oxford, they lacked a personal faith in Christ's saving grace.

However, after a failed missionary trip to Georgia and through much fellowship with some Moravian believers, on May 21, 1738, Wesley believed in the efficacy of the blood of the Lord Jesus and was "at peace with God."

For more than five decades, Wesley was a leader in kindling the flame of revival that spread throughout eighteenth-century England, by preaching the gospel of Jesus Christ. Convinced that what people sing is what they believe, he daily gave himself to composing thousands of poems and hymns, thus enabling generations of Christians to give voice to their faith and to render their highest praises to the Lord Jesus Christ.

Charles Wesley died on Saturday, March 29, 1788. He had spent his entire life proclaiming:

Behold the Lamb!

And Can It Be?

Loving Desperation

With my soul I have desired
You in the night, yes,
by my spirit within me I will
seek You early... *Isaiah 26:9*

Where Is He, My Jesus?

HOWARD HIGASHI
1937–1998

LOVING DESPERATION

Without faith it is impossible to please Him, for he who comes to God must believe that He is, and that He is a rewarder of those who diligently seek Him. (Hebrews 11:6)

The gospel in its simplest form tells the story of how God loved man; the account of Mary the Magdalene tells the story of how she loved God. We must tell the story of both—of the Lord's loving us and of our loving Him in return. His love for us drew Him out of the heavens to dwell with us as our Immanuel. Our love for Him draws us out of the world that we may receive an ever-increasing transformation that includes the ultimate satisfaction of becoming a part of the Bride of Christ.

Mary the Magdalene might represent any believer. Though she was hopelessly possessed of seven demons, one word from the Savior freed her. Her initial thankfulness and appreciation grew into love and adoration as she beheld the Prince of Peace daily denying Himself for the benefit of others. She became a testimony to the reality that one who is forgiven much loves much. We also have been greatly forgiven and should love Him likewise.

Why, then, would we wait to love Him? Physical invisibility cannot hide His practical and spiritual presence from the loving heart's eye of faith. During this age, His Bride is being prepared to participate in the greatest enjoyment of that loving relationship with her Bridegroom. Like Mary, whose heart soared upon hearing the freshly resurrected Christ speak her name, our hearts will rise as if on eagle's wings when that same love is kindled within us!

We may entrust our time, our considerations, and our innermost secrets to Him Who is always waiting for us to draw near. May we learn to desperately seek Him as Mary did! He Himself is the greatest reward a seeking heart could ever find!

Where Is He, My Jesus?

Where Is He, My Jesus?

Verse One

I do not know where they have laid Him;
Why has the stone been rolled back
    from the tomb?
They must have taken Him away!
Oh! Where is He?

Verse Two

Disciples came to see the empty tomb,
Why have they gone so soon
    to their own homes?
They sadly left, not seeing Him;
But where's my Lord?

> *Chorus—*
> Where is He, my Jesus?
> Where is He, my Beloved?
> Where is He Whom my soul doth love?
> Jesus, my Love, I just want You.

Verse Three

My heart is broken from my deepest need.
Don't ask me, angels, why I'm weeping.
Nothing but Jesus fills my inner being.
Oh! Where's my Love?

Verse Four

Someone is standing right behind me—
It's just the gardener, I can barely see.
Sir, if you carried Him away ...
Oh! Where is He?

Chorus—

Where is He, my Jesus?
Where is He, my Beloved?
Tell me where you have laid Him
And I'll carry Him away,
I'll carry Him away.

Verse Five

And then I heard a Voice say, "Mary,"
That sweetest voice that penetrated me.
It is the voice of my Beloved!
Jesus, my Love!

> *Chorus—*
> I have found my Jesus!
> I have found my Beloved!
> I have found Whom my soul doth love,
> Jesus, my Love, I just love You!

Verse Six

But Jesus asked me not to touch Him yet;
He must ascend first to the Father,
And to My Father and your Father,
To My God, and your God.

> *Chorus—*
> Go and tell My brothers,
> I ascend to the Father,
> To My Father and your Father,
> And My God and your God,
> Go tell My brothers.

WHERE IS HE, MY JESUS?

Loving Desperation

"LORD, TO WHOM SHALL WE GO?"

The unexpected capture, trial, and crucifixion of the Lord Jesus Christ stunned His followers. They had placed all their hopes in Him, only to see them crushed before their eyes. As Mary the Magdalene lingered at the tomb, weeping in sorrow, how bewildering the events of the last few hours must have been.

There was Judas' traitorous betrayal, Christ's arrest, and the scattering of those closest to Him. Next came the consecutive trials—a compound conspiracy between the embittered religious leaders and the Roman occupiers they otherwise despised—all contrived to murder the Lord of Life. Their diabolical plotting would turn the curious crowd into a murderous mob, inciting them to chant for the release of yet another murderer, Barabbas, in exchange for a judgment against the guileless Shepherd of men and Friend of sinners. During this insidious process, the Lord Jesus was spit upon, cruelly mocked, and savagely beaten. And what is more, during the night, between the two trials, He was denied three times by His boldest disciple.

With more noise of vile hatred, the throng proceeded to Golgotha, where Jesus' hands and feet were nailed to the cross, and the thorny crown for "The King of the Jews" was plunged into His brow. On the cross, His six hours of utter agony finally ended in death. And what of the strange daytime darkness accompanied by an earthquake? So many horrifying and illogical events came so quickly against this most noble, kind, and loving One!

Mary's desperate seeking of the Lord and her reward of the very presence of the resurrected Christ are wonderfully echoed in this song by Howard Higashi, also a seeker and lover of the Lord Jesus.

large group of college-age students who had devoted their lives to Christ were seated before Howard Higashi, whose words of testimony were loosed like an arrow toward the target of their hearts. They paid rapt attention to him because he was a man who loved them. He wanted them to "realize that God's whole burden is just for mankind." Higashi encouraged them to not waste their lives in distractions away from God, particularly in this world's most natural allurements. He imparted to them the biblical insight that in the most holy sense, a divine romance exists between God and man. He told them the Creator longs that each "person will receive the Triune God" and that "everything else that is happening on the earth is temporary and just vanity." He stood before them as a spiritual father who had spent almost thirty years cultivating his *own* loving relationship with the Lord.

Where Is He, My Jesus?

The Bright Dawning

Of Japanese ancestry, Howard Higashi grew up in Hawaii amid a peaceful environment, surrounded by nature's beauty and bounty. His family lived a simple, relatively carefree life. Generational practice caused his family to continue in the tradition of Buddhist worship as a matter of course. One of Howard's childhood memories was of bowing to a statue while he nestled securely between his parents.

He followed various pagan practices well into adulthood, never having seen a single Bible in his parents' home.

Howard's father's early death caused him to become troubled by the fear of death and his lack of knowledge of God. He moved to Los Angeles and got married, thinking, *Well, maybe she will help to make me happy.* But still his inward thirst for God continued unabated. He sensed a gnawing emptiness, which he tried to fill with music, sports, friends, and entertainment—all to no avail. However, through a fellow

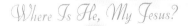

Where Is He, My Jesus?

college student's burden to share the gospel, Higashi found faith in Jesus Christ at the age of thirty-one and, thereafter, poured out his love on the One Who had given meaning to his life. The poetry he wrote and sang to the Lord continually released his inner joy and helped him express his love of Christ to many.

Higashi's taste for the world's music profoundly changed after falling in love with Christ. Before his conversion, he was always playing his ukulele. However, upon finding the Savior, Howard "gave up all his singing, all his past life, and his favorite instruments, to be consecrated for the Lord." Howard's wife spoke of him as having a musical gift given "in resurrection because he was willing to just drop it all, and then the Lord brought him His songs." Howard testified, "As soon as I got saved, I began to sing the songs on the blood to wash away all the other things." The natural enjoyments previously so attractive—even the music he liked most—faded into oblivion with the bright dawning of Christ's love in his life.

Each morning around five o'clock, Howard Higashi would rise from sleep and fellowship with the Savior he adored. Praise, and then poetry, spontaneously flowed from his joy, and he would find himself worshiping in song. The words often came effortlessly, but never accidentally. Higashi exercised his spirit in prayer and in the Word to plunge

Where Is He, My Jesus?

himself into the wellspring of God's love—endeavoring to keep his heart open to be freshly touched by the Lord's speaking. In response, his deepest feelings toward Christ found expression in the poems he wrote. Such was the case in this spiritual song, "Where Is He, My Jesus?"

NO REST AT THE SEPULCHER

Through this particular poem, Higashi brings us into the ageless story of Mary the Magdalene, from whom the Lord had cast out seven demons. Having been forgiven and set free, she determined to follow the Lord along with many others as they traveled from city to city announcing the gospel of the kingdom. The Gospel of John contains the historical record of the awful betrayal, mock trial, and execution of the Lord. It also vividly portrays the poignant moments that followed Christ's crucifixion, wherein John described Mary's desperate pursuit and rapturous discovery of her resurrected Lord.

Higashi's poem opens with Mary's heartfelt cry: "I do not know where they have laid Him." There was no rest for her on that dark night as the world of guilty men still slept like the stone upon His sepulcher. We do not know from the Gospel accounts how many seekers of the Lord visited His tomb, but not one is recorded as remaining—except Mary, who simply would not leave until she had ascertained where her Lord, her Love, was. Indeed, to adequately grasp why Mary's seeking of the Lord was so deeply inspiring, it is important to note that *Mary alone lingered at the tomb*. She had

Mary Magdalene: "I have seen the Lord!"

I HAVE FOUND MY LOVE,
HE HAS RISEN FROM THE DEAD.
NOW OUR JESUS IS ALIVE,
I HAVE SEEN HIM, SEEN HIM!
I LOVE HIM!

HOWARD HIGASHI

Where Is He, My Jesus?

found the tomb's sealing stone rolled from the entrance, only to reveal that His body was not there! Who had taken Him away? Her pain was more than anxious concern, it was panic— her Lord was gone! She had been robbed of all that was dear to her! She rushed to tell the disciples that the tomb was empty, and they ran to see for themselves. Then they simply melted away to their own homes to ponder what had become of their Master.

But Mary, in her loving, desperate pursuit, would not be satisfied by mere facts. She stayed at the tomb and wept; neither family nor friends, neither home nor country could give her solace. Who cared for angels, bright raiment, or heaven itself—if it should descend—if He were gone? Evidence of the resurrection? If so, where *was* He? She needed *Him* Who had first loved her.

THAT SWEETEST VOICE

This song poses her anxious question: "Where is He, my Jesus? Where is He, my Beloved?" Mary wept: "My heart is broken from my deepest need." No one and nothing else could replace her profound loss. There was no comfort in taking steps that would further distance her from where His body had been laid—only to languish in isolation from Him. Suddenly, Mary had an awareness that "Someone" was standing right behind her! The supposed gardener asked her why she was weeping, and whom was she seeking? Mary, desperately desiring to find the Lord's body, cried out that she herself would carry Him away!

Then, He spoke her name—"*Mary.*" Instantly she recognized His voice and turned to Him! Heartbroken weeping turned into rejoicing at the sight of Him, the now resurrected Lord! She had found Him! Once more she heard what Higashi described as "that sweetest voice." When the Good Shepherd calls His sheep by name, they know Him and follow Him. Throughout the centuries, many

Where Is He, My Jesus?

Mary Magdalene: "They have taken away my Lord."

WHAT WERE THOSE ANGEL-
FORMS TO HER,
THEIR RADIANT FORMS AND
RAIMENT WHITE,
IF DEAD WITHIN A SEPULCHER
HE LAY, HIMSELF THE LIFE AND LIGHT?

ELISABETH RUNDLE CHARLES

who love Christ have read this account in the New Testament and have substituted their own names in place of Mary's.

Higashi also knew what it meant to desperately seek the Lord. Prayer was not mere duty to him, but a means for fresh contact with his dear Savior. His wife, Lily, told others, "I know he had a very deep prayer life. Sometimes I would open the door and find him kneeling down and praying. He prayed a lot before he contacted people." Beginning each day simply and purely loving Jesus, Higashi added the weight of his prayers to the accomplishment of God's purpose here on earth. Through his experience with the One indwelling his spirit, Higashi enjoyed the very same Christ in resurrection Whom Mary had found that day.

The Lord intentionally appeared first to Mary. Why? Only Mary had remained—waiting and hoping. Those who had come to the tomb that day left to go home, and though the Lord equally loved them, He did not appear to them. *What caused Mary to remain?* The record makes it clear: Her fervent, relentless love of Jesus kept her there. And how very great was her reward—she was the first person on earth to see Christ in resurrection!

"GO AND TELL MY BROTHERS"

Then and there, what did the Lord Jesus commission her to do? He entrusted her to tell the disciples a most personal and reassuring

word—
a declaration
to His people that
their relationship with Him
would become even more intimate than
before His departure in death and return in
resurrection. He was no longer merely their
Friend, but the Lord Jesus now emphatically
addressed them as His brothers!

Through His resurrection, they would be
born anew with the Father's divine life, a new
creation in Christ! That is why the Lord sent
Mary to assure them that His God was now
their God and His Father was their Father; they
were all holy brothers in a new race of men,
actually able to have God's life and nature
within them through regeneration. As earlier
prophesied, the Lord had fallen into the
ground and died as a "grain of wheat." But the
power of resurrection in this seed of life multi-
plied to create many duplicate grains, in these
early disciples and in many more besides!

It is easy to see why Howard Higashi, having a kindred spirit and heart with Mary,
would write this song to give further voice to
her message, for he often told young believers
about their wonderful change in status—they
were sinners, yet they had become sons of
God. He reminded them, "God chose us in
eternity. He separated us from our mother's
womb. He knew everything that we were in—
what family we were born into, what school
we would go to—and who knows how many
things He had to do to protect us?" But, as part
of Adam's fallen race, we "became corrupted,
constituted with sin. Yet His choosing us never
changed." And we were chosen not only to be
friends of God, but born again to become sons
of God and brothers of Jesus Christ!

Where Is He, My Jesus?

The principle in Mary's story is very significant: The resurrected Lord reveals Himself more to those who love Him much. Higashi's wife recalled that her husband's concern was to help believers love their Lord more intensely and consecrate themselves to Him more deeply. He longed that all would just come back to their first love, to Jesus Christ Himself. This poem and the music Higashi set it to certainly accomplishes his intended desire: to draw its listeners to open their hearts to the Lord of Love and to enter into a lifelong relationship of love with the Savior-God—just as Mary did, and just as he did.

Howard Higashi's song expresses that there is no joy comparable to having the glory of the resurrected person of the Lord Jesus break upon one who is gripped in death's dark night. Thus, for all loving Christians, the resurrected Christ, Who is our life, is here and now, real and personal.

Lord Jesus,

I want to desperately seek You as Mary did! I want to love You with a pure and loving heart. Lord, appear to me as You did to Mary! I am listening for Your voice. I want to linger and fellowship with You. Make me desperate for You. Remind me to tell You more each day, "Lord Jesus, I love You!"

Amen

Where Is He, My Jesus?

Howard Higashi
1937–1998

February 28, 1937, Howard Higashi was born to a Hawaiian sugar plantation foreman and his wife. Little did these parents imagine that their newborn infant was destined to become a melodious servant of Christ. Higashi was born a third-generation Hawaiian of Japanese Buddhist ancestry. Growing up enjoying the easygoing environment of the island seemed unlikely to prepare his heart to be a desperate seeker of God.

Nevertheless, paradise seemed to end when the father he adored had several heart attacks. Higashi drained his savings to fly back and forth from college in California to be with his father, who died at the age of fifty-two. For the first time, Higashi began to question the meaning of life. He married Lily Agena in 1965, which brought some comfort to him.

In 1968, Higashi met a Christian who was called by the Lord to go back to college for the gospel's sake. This student's daily living touched Higashi, who received the Lord that year when he was thirty-one. He had a dynamic salvation that opened his wife to the gospel; she received the Lord soon afterward. Higashi later obtained a degree to become a high-school math teacher, but he chose to respond to the Lord's call by faith instead.

The Higashis were instrumental in reaching hundreds of college students and many relatives with the gospel of Christ. Higashi spent the rest of his life laboring in the gospel from campus to campus, shepherding others, writing spiritual songs, and ministering the truth in order to build up the Body of Christ. He was called home to Christ on November 27, 1998, at the age of sixty-one.

Where Is He, My Jesus?

Inner Abundance

 You open Your hand and satisfy

the desire of every living thing....

The LORD is near to all

who call upon Him,

to all who call upon Him

in truth. *Psalm 145:16, 18*

Satisfied

CLARA TEAR WILLIAMS
1858–1937

INNER ABUNDANCE

O God, You are my God; early will I seek You; my soul thirsts for You;
my flesh longs for You in a dry and thirsty land where there is no water. (Psalm 63:1)

Jesus stood and cried out, saying,
"If anyone thirsts, let him come to Me and drink." (John 7:37b)

In the chorus of this beautiful hymn, Clara Tear Williams joyfully exclaims, "Hallelujah! I have found Him!" She had discovered the One Who could satisfy her deepest need. Not a philosophy, a religion, or even a better way—she had found God Himself.

In her quest to find meaning in life, Clara had experienced the familiar but deep disappointments of fleeting and shallow entertainment, empty accomplishments, and unfulfilled ambitions. A whole world of those desires, however innocently pursued, could not satisfy her sense of longing "for a drink from some cool spring" to "quench the burning of the thirst ... within."

In spite of our fallen nature within and the corrupting ways of the world without, there is a yearning for God deep within us—He designed us so! His Spirit witnesses with our spirit, assuring us that only God as the genuine food and drink can satisfy.

When we receive Jesus Christ as Clara did, we also will rejoice that our Redeemer is a "well of water, ever springing"; the "Bread of life, so rich and free"; and "untold wealth that never faileth." Hallelujah! We have found Him!

Satisfied

Satisfied

Verse One

All my life long I had panted
For a drink from some cool spring,
That I hoped would quench the burning
Of the thirst I felt within.

Chorus

Hallelujah! I have found Him
Whom my soul so long has craved!
Jesus satisfies my longings;
Thro' His life I now am saved.

Verse Two

Feeding on the husks around me,
Till my strength was almost gone,
Longed my soul for something better,
Only still to hunger on.

Verse Three

Poor I was, and sought for riches,
Something that would satisfy,
But the dust I gathered round me
Only mocked my soul's sad cry.

Verse Four

Well of water, ever springing,
Bread of life, so rich and free,
Untold wealth that never faileth,
My Redeemer is to me.

SATISFIED

Inner Abundance

SADDLEBAGS FOR A PILLOW

After their dramatic conversion to Christ in 1738, Charles and John Wesley began "circuit-riding," traversing Great Britain on horseback to preach the gospel and strengthen believers. They carried little more than their greatest treasures— the Bible and their book of hymns. This practice was faithfully continued in the United States, characterized by what Peter Cartwright wrote in his autobiography: A circuit rider endured "storms of wind, hail, snow, and rain; climbed hills and mountains, traversed valleys, plunged through swamps, swollen streams, lay out all night, wet, weary, and hungry, ... slept with his saddle blanket for a bed, his saddle bags for a pillow." Though often very young, they were truly dedicated: "Of those who died up to 1847, nearly half were less than 30 years old." Clara Tear Williams was also a circuit-riding preacher of the gospel of Jesus Christ.

After a gospel meeting in Troy, Ohio, one of the helpers was requested to write a poem for a new hymnbook. Going back to her room that night, Clara Tear Williams began reflecting on her satisfaction in Christ and His abundant provision in her life and quickly wrote a poem before retiring to bed. The very next morning, Ralph E. Hudson, the compiler of the new hymnbook, wrote an accompanying tune. Thus, the jubilant hymn "Satisfied" was published, providing a sweet opportunity for Christians to express abundant satisfaction with their Savior in song.

While singing this hymn, one might assume that the author had spent many long years in roaming the earth, panting "for a drink from some cool spring." But Clara Tear Williams had heeded the exhortation from Ecclesiastes to remember God in the days of her youth! She was still in her teens when she penned this sweet, insightful poem, often referred to by the exultant first line of the chorus, "Hallelujah! I have found Him!" But for Clara, her title

Satisfied

"Satisfied" tells it all. She had discovered this profound truth—mankind was made for God and is truly content only with Him. She "found Him"—a Person—Jesus Christ! He became her "well of water, ever springing" and the "Bread of life, so rich and free"!

YOUTHFUL PURSUIT OF CHRIST

Growing up on a family farm in the mid-1800s and having been trained in a manner that cultivated a sensitive conscience, Clara was only thirteen when she felt she was headed in the wrong direction and that her heart was growing harder and harder. She knew that if she did not soon come genuinely into submission to the Lord, she might never! She stated, "One night the matter was settled and as I started up the aisle toward the altar the love of God came into my heart."

Clara's salvation experience was not overly emotional; she characterized her rebirth as not so noticeably *strong* as it was *real*. Afterward, she saw the evidence within her heart in her newfound love for God's children. She testified, "Before, I wanted to shun them, now my heart was drawn toward them. 'We know that we have passed from death unto life because we love the brothers.'"

However, it was not as though Clara were exempt from youthful folly and passions. For most, the world's allure never beckons more strongly than during those particularly susceptible teen years. As a teen, she confessed that she "failed to keep the blessing of the Lord and a place of amusement became more attractive." But the Lord had not forsaken her. Rather, He was moving within her, allowing her to realize that the worldly enticements would only leave her with a burning thirst. In vain, she tried to satisfy her hunger by "feeding on the husks around" her.

But Clara came to a definite point when she felt she had been lured and cheated enough by the world's deceits.

◦ ─≪≫─ ◦

FLOOD OF GLORY

After a meeting when Clara was seventeen, she heard the Lord's voice calling her to a higher level:

As we drove from the church and I looked back at the unworldly appearing [gospel] workers ..., knowing as I did that they were despised, the question came forcibly: Would I be willing to give up the world with its fashions and pleasures and fully follow the Lord? My heart responded, "Yes," and there flowed through my being a flood of glory that was inexpressible. Not a word was spoken, and while I believed I had received the cleansing of my heart, I was kept from testifying to it.

Nevertheless, her pastor perceptively noted that she had "taken advanced ground." Clara stated, "From that time I believe Jesus was first in my life."

Her young acquaintances also noticed the change in Clara, and as one would expect, it was not always well received. Her popularity declined, but she overcame that oft-enslaving idol of youth—the admiration and acceptance of her peers. She remembered how "the trifling giddy young people" at school no longer liked her, and she suffered "some small persecutions." How blessed she was to learn their "true loyalties" so soon.

Early in Clara's Christian life, a devastating event occurred, triggering a crisis of consecration. Clara had been provided an opportunity to share Christ's saving grace with two of her classmates. Though desirous to do so, she did not, for her "tongue seemed tied." Shortly thereafter she heard shocking news that her two friends "were both in eternity." She was stricken with regret and turned desperately to seek the Lord.

Clara's Wonderful Counselor intervened in the resultant struggle in her heart through touching words from the hymn "I Need Thee

Every Hour." She said, "The Holy Spirit burnt into my soul my awful need of *His abiding presence....* From that time I knew what it was to 'hunger and thirst after righteousness.'" How gracious the Lord was to turn a great loss and her accompanying sense of abject failure into eternal gain.

CHRIST MAKES HIS HOME

Clara had aspirations for her future: "My ambition was to make teaching my life work." She felt teaching would supply security and held the prospect of getting the education that her poor health in childhood had prevented. And it would satisfy her desire to "dress well" and "associate with nice, intelligent people." However, for Clara, attaining these goals became a subtle temptation. Her dilemma was one every serious pursuer of Christ has faced. If she were to give herself and her dreams to the Lord without reservation, He may require *everything.*

Clara explained, "While I had given myself to the Lord, it now seemed infinitely more to consent to His taking possession, and control of my entire being." She described her struggle: "Was I willing to be separate from this proud

Why Pray?

HAVING YIELDED HER PLANS FOR TEACHING TO THE LORD, ONE LAST OPPORTUNITY TO FULFILL HER EARTHLY DREAMS PRESENTED ITSELF:

AT ONE TIME A GENTLEMAN ... OFFERED ME A POSITION AS TEACHER WHICH WAS QUITE TEMPTING. I TOLD HIM I WOULD SEND HIM A REPLY IN A FEW DAYS. I WENT TO MY ROOM AND MY KNEES, WHEN THE LORD SAID TO ME, "HAVEN'T I TOLD YOU WHAT I WANT YOU TO DO? WHY PRAY?" I IMMEDIATELY WENT OUT AND GAVE MY ANSWER TO THE MAN WHO HAD NOT YET DRIVEN OUT OF THE YARD.

～ CTW

wicked world, and live only to please God? To be like Him, despised and rejected of men? It seemed for two days and nights I could not say yes. The suggestion came that I had at times been much blessed of the Lord and had been living a good life, why not be content?" Upon quenching that fiery dart, Clara would not draw back from obedience: "I came to a point where the matter had to be settled." Her struggle ceased—she relinquished her future plans and ambitions, giving her life unreservedly to spreading the gospel full-time.

While waiting for the Lord's direction, Clara continued teaching. However, she soon suffered severe illness. She wrote, "A cough was sapping my strength; my arms became so weak that I was obliged to rest before I could finish combing my hair, and some of the time in school I could scarcely speak above a whisper." Shortly thereafter, she was diagnosed with the dreaded tuberculosis. She later said, "My family despaired of my life, but I knew that the Lord had work for me to do and I would recover."

During her long convalescence, Clara learned how to enjoy the Lord more consistently day by day and to be satisfied with Christ alone. She related, "My full heart found increasing expression in song, prayer, and testimony." When her health was restored, she began to serve in gospel meetings and soon wrote "Satisfied."

Clara's lifetime of satisfaction in Christ overflowed to others as she traversed the Ohio Valley, the Alleghenies, the Catskills, and the Adirondack Mountains, singing and speaking the gospel in church meetings, camp meetings, and serving as a circuit-riding preacher. Clara married William H. Williams when she was thirty-six, and together they traveled sharing the gospel of Jesus Christ for the rest of their lives.

If we allow the Lord to reign in our hearts, He can do amazing, forever meaningful work. In her youth, Clara Tear Williams learned that Jesus would always satisfy her longings. Her hymn "Satisfied" has been echoed by many a Christian heart ever since.

Lord Jesus,

Give me the desire to drink of You to quench my thirst again and again. You are the "Bread of life, so rich and free" that satisfies my hunger every day. For my poverty, You are my "untold wealth" that never fails! Oh, what a Redeemer You are! Gain my heart at this age, in my stage, and in all my circumstances.

Amen

Satisfied

Clara Tear Williams

1858–1937

Clara Tear Williams was born on September 22, 1858, near Painesville, Ohio. She grew up on the homestead inherited from her Christian ancestors who emigrated from the Isle of Man—where they had heard John Wesley preach. At the age of thirteen, "the love of God" came into her heart. In her teens, Clara increasingly consecrated her life to the Lord, yielding her future into His hands.

During her late teens, Clara began assisting others in holding gospel meetings, at which time she penned "Satisfied." Later, she traveled and preached from town to town as a circuit rider in several states, filling a spiritual void among God's people.

In May 1895 at the age of thirty-six, she married William H. Williams. He had been a profane, godless young man, but after turning thirty, he had a profound reconsideration of his life and came under intense conviction of his sinful state. A timely word from a faithful Christian leader drove William to go home, pray, and confess his sins. Pacing the floor, he flung open the door of his heart, believed into Christ, and was saved.

This spiritually well-matched couple gave their lives to the Lord's work. William faithfully earned their living, both as a mill foreman and a school janitor. At other times, he and Clara were circuit riders together. They had three daughters.

Clara served with her husband until his death on May 17, 1934, at the age of seventy-nine. Clara went to be with the Lord on July 1, 1937, at the age of seventy-eight. In addition to leading many individuals to the Lord, Clara wrote the enduring hymn "Satisfied" for future generations to enjoy Christ.

Satisfied

Sweet Path

 THIS IS THE MEANING OF CHRISTIANITY;

IT IS THE BREATH OF A NEW NATURE;

IT IS THE TRANSLATION OF THE SOUL INTO

A HIGHER UNIVERSE AND

A LOFTIER SCALE OF BEING.

Albert Benjamin Simpson

I Am Crucified with Christ

ALBERT BENJAMIN SIMPSON
1843–1919

A Sweet Path to Glory

I have been crucified with Christ; it is no longer I who live,
but Christ lives in me. (Galatians 2:20a)

Therefore, if anyone is in Christ, he is a new creation. (2 Corinthians 5:17a)

All believers in Christ have been bought with the precious Redeemer's blood and were transferred into the realm of light and life in God's dear Son. Christ Jesus carried with Him every member of the corrupted race to the cross and terminated each of them there. What relief from bondage Albert Benjamin Simpson saw in a cross that annihilated every resultant problem from Adam's fall; he saw no dread in this kind of death, declaring, "Oh! It is so sweet to die with Christ." It is *only* at this pleasant place—the cross—that the believer can be rid of the "world, and self, and sin."

The cross is "our path to glory," opening to us the "mystery hid from ancient ages." Simpson discovered "the secret of the holy" is "not our holiness, but Him." The secret of living the Christian life is to *not* live it. Our dying to self allows the only One Who ever could live the Christian life to live it within us, for "He lives and reigns within"! "The cross hath set me free," and now "it is so sweet to live with Christ."

Living in the new creation is infinitely better than merely existing in the old. It is a good thing to be crucified with Christ, for only dead men are free from the old life of self and sin, and only those in His resurrection life are truly alive to God. When the accomplished fact of self's death becomes our reality, the heavenly doors to a new life in Christ fly open. When self goes out, Christ comes in, and how sweet is this path to life and glory!

I Am Crucified with Christ

I Am Crucified with Christ

Verse One

I am crucified with Christ,
And the cross hath set me free;
I have ris'n again with Christ,
And He lives and reigns in me.

Chorus:
Oh! it is so sweet to die with Christ,
To the world, and self, and sin;
Oh! it is so sweet to live with Christ,
As He lives and reigns within.

Verse Two

Mystery hid from ancient ages!
But at length to faith made plain:
Christ in me the Hope of Glory,
Tell it o'er and o'er again.

Verse Three

This the secret nature hideth,
Harvest grows from buried grain;
A poor tree with better grafted,
Richer, sweeter life doth gain.

Verse Four

This the secret of the holy,
Not our holiness, but Him;
O Lord! empty us and fill us,
With Thy fulness to the brim.

Verse Five

This the balm for pain and sickness,
Just to all our strength to die,
And to find His life and fulness,
All our being's need supply.

Verse Six

This the story of the Master,
Thru the Cross, He reached the Throne,
And like Him our path to glory,
Ever leads through death alone.

I AM CRUCIFIED
WITH CHRIST

A Sweet Path to Glory

A CRY IN THE WILDERNESS

During the second half of the nineteenth century, North America was the battleground of differing "gospels" among the professing community. Within a number of denominations, the practice of the Christian faith was becoming institutionalized, its purity diluted with modernism. Many clergymen, seminary theologians, and authors seemed eager even to capitulate on the Bible's authority and accuracy. In part, this compromise was due to the struggle to accommodate both Darwinism and the rise of science as a Western religion.

To fill a void they had helped to make, these leaders encouraged their followers to find purpose in the social gospel of behavioral modification and humanitarian works. All of these factors reduced the emphasis on Christ's redemption by grace, thus diminishing basic orthodoxy. Reaction to this spiritual decline was seen in a powerful burst of gospel activity by many nonsectarian evangelists, including D. L. Moody and R. A. Torrey.

A. B. Simpson also spent his lifetime in fervent gospel preaching and in seeking to unite denominations for worldwide evangelization while learning to depend on the Lord for everything.

_L_ate at night during a fierce storm, a prominent gentleman heard a knock at his door. He invited the unanticipated visitor, Albert Benjamin Simpson, within to dry off by the fire in the study. Simpson spoke from an open heart to express his great concern for his host's eternal destiny—a topic to which the host had given little prior consideration. Deeply touched by Simpson's loving concern to seek him amid the raging tempest and now convicted of his heart's condition, the host turned to the Lord.

IF THE LORD SO WILLS

It was on the fifteenth of December, a cold winter day in 1843 on Prince Edward Island, that Albert was born, the fourth of nine children, to James and Jane Simpson. Albert's mother requested of the Lord "that the boy might be a minister or missionary," cautiously adding, "If the Lord so wills, and he lives to grow up and is so inclined." She immersed young Albert in the noblest literature and poetry; her "aspirations,

I Am Crucified with Christ

her soaring imagination" became his as well. His father was a "Presbyterian elder of the old school." He believed in all the "principles of a well-ordered Puritan household" and "the efficacy of the rod."

Of his early influences, Simpson wrote, "I cannot say I wholly regret the somewhat stern mould in which my early life was shaped," for it "threw over my youthful spirit a natural horror of evil things which often safeguarded me afterwards when thrown as a young man amid the temptations of the world." In fact, young Albert wanted to become a minister of the gospel. However, funds were limited, so his father quietly informed Albert that it would be his duty to stay at home on the farm while his elder brother went to college to enter the ministry. At the tender age of nearly fourteen, he stated,

> I can still feel the lump that rose in my throat as I stammered out my acquiescence. Then I ventured with broken words and stammering tongue to plead that they would consent to my getting an education if I could work it out without asking anything from them but their approval and blessing.... I remember the quiet trembling tones with which my father received my request and said, "God bless you, my boy."
>
> So the struggle began, and I shall never cease to thank God that it was a hard one.

To enter the ministry, Simpson had to become a candidate for examination by the presbytery, so he was tutored in Greek, Latin, and advanced mathematics. Later, he traveled to study at Chatham High School, nine miles from his home on foot or horseback. Since he was of a weakened constitution, the strain caused him to become a "physical wreck." Simpson's physical distress "predisposed him toward despair," worsened because he was not regenerated! He explained, "I had no personal hope in Christ. My whole religious training had left me without any conception of the sweet and simple Gospel of Jesus Christ. The God I knew was a being of great severity." This narrow and extreme view

DARE TO BELIEVE

While glancing through the library of his former minister and tutor, Simpson came across "an old musty volume called *Marshall's Gospel Mystery of Sanctification.*" As he scanned its pages, a sentence, "which opened ... the gates of life eternal," caught his eye:

The first good work you will ever perform is to believe on the Lord Jesus Christ. Until you do this, all your works, prayers, tears, and good resolutions are vain. To believe on the Lord Jesus is just to believe that He saves you according to His Word, that He receives and saves you here and now, for He has said —"Him that cometh to me I will in no wise cast out."

of an austere God caused "the accumulated terrors of a multitude of books and sermons on total depravity and the damnation of the non-elect [to] roar out upon him like a lion from the thicket and throw him into mortal panic for his dying soul," stirring him to seek salvation with all his heart.

I Am Crucified with Christ

He fell to his knees and cried out to the Lord Jesus to save him:

I come the best I can, and I dare to believe that Thou dost receive me and save me, and that I am now Thy child, forgiven and saved simply because I have taken Thee at Thy word.

Afterward, Simpson felt he had the "supreme joy of a soul in its earliest love." In response to this joy, he wrote and formally sealed his "Solemn Covenant" with the Lord—one he would keep with him and renew at pivotal times in his life—which included this telling line:

I yield myself unto Thee as one alive from the dead, for time and eternity. Take me and use me entirely for Thy glory.

At age seventeen, Simpson earned a teacher's certificate and taught in county schools until he entered Knox College in Toronto. True to his plan to "work out" his education, he put himself through college by tutoring, preaching, and winning scholarships. Although unquestionably redeemed through faith in Christ, he said, "My religious life was chiefly that of duty, with little joy or fellowship.... I had not yet learned the secret of the indwelling Christ." After graduating in 1865, Simpson began to serve as a pastor in Hamilton, Ontario. That same year, he married Margaret Henry, who had "all the quiet dignity and resourcefulness" to support Dr. Simpson throughout a long and eventful life.

A few years into their marriage, Albert and Margaret suffered the great loss of their little toddler Melville. His last poignant words in the arms of his father were, "Take me to Mamma." Once in her arms, the little one quoted the Scriptures, "Abide in Me and I in you," as his mother had taught him, and then he died. Mrs. Simpson said later that "this was the first message that ever sank deeply into her heart" and that the words of her dying child prepared her for an ever-deepening experience of abiding in Christ.

THE BENDED KNEE PREVAILS

In January 1874, Simpson's second chapter of ministry began in Louisville, Kentucky, and he gave his pledge to the congregation to preach "Jesus only." Even though it was ten years after the Civil War ended, Louisville's churches were still beset with smoldering hostility between Northern and Southern sympathizers. Seen as a neutral Canadian, Simpson invited all of Louisville's church leaders to his home with a goal of reconciliation and revival. Knowing that the bended knee is the most prevailing denial of self, he insisted that they first engage in prayer. God softened their hearts, and as repenting commenced, a tearful reconciliation began among all but one stubborn attendant. Afterward, revival swept over Louisville, and hundreds were saved.

A specially invited speaker in the revival, Major D. W. Whittle, deeply affected Dr. Simpson through his depth of experience and joy in Christ. As Simpson listened night after night to the preaching,

a vast uneasiness came over his heart; the hyphenated self-qualities [of] self-love, self-confidence, self-seeking, all that Adam-begotten brood of illegitimate soul children which inhabited his life, began to make him sick utterly.

Driven to his room to pray, Simpson yielded himself to the Lord in utter abandonment.

As expressed in his song "I Am Crucified with Christ," the world and all its offerings and the self with all its private interests died to him that night. Still greatly desiring more power in his Christian service, Simpson later sought counsel from "an old, experienced friend," who shared with him this faithful word:

All you need ... to make your life a power for God is to be annihilated.

Simpson later reflected,

The fact is the shock of that message almost annihilated me for the time, but before God's faithful discipline was through, I had learned ... that I am not sufficient to think anything of myself.

This counsel led to Simpson's life-altering realization that "dying with Christ" simply released the indwelling Christ to be his life lived out day by day!

THE LIFE OF THE VINE OVERFLOWS

Simpson clearly saw the critical distinction between the work of regeneration and the Holy Spirit's indwelling the human spirit:

"The one is like the building of the house; the other the owner moving in and making it his own personal residence."

However, Simpson did not consider his spiritual life with Christ as the *end*, but rather as the *means* to minister Christ to individuals, cities, and ultimately to nations. In fact, "the inward pressure" to evangelize worldwide was "being born out of a heart big with love for God and the perishing world." In 1879, when the Thirteenth Street Church in New York City urged him to come, he felt God had given the opportunity to carry out his burden in that gateway to the world.

Simpson was greatly used in bringing the gospel to both the upscale congregation and the neglected of society. After more than a hundred poor Italian immigrants were won to Christ through his preaching on the streets, the church leaders pointed out that the new converts were not "social equals" and might feel more "at home" among their "own kind."

Although Simpson had served for two happy years "with this noble people," he realized that "it would be difficult for them to adjust themselves to the radical and aggressive measures to which God was leading" him. After a week of fervent prayer, he asked to be released "for the purpose of preaching the Gospel to the masses." Resigning meant giving up a comfortable salary with which to support his family of six children, a decision that astonished the church leaders. Visiting the parsonage the next day, they "offered their condolences" to his wife, saying they felt they "had come to his funeral." Nevertheless, Simpson obeyed the Lord.

Simpson immediately started evangelical meetings, the first attended by only seven. They opened their Bibles to "who hath despised the day of small things?" Then, knowing their need of the Holy Spirit for the work, they knelt and thanked God that they were few, poor, and weak. Within eight years, a six-story building was built, which included a bookstore, a missionary training center, and a large meeting hall to evangelize the masses. Consequently, hundreds of kindred missionaries of the gospel were raised up through his labors, and vast multitudes came to Christ.

Following the apostle Paul's pattern, Simpson was obedient to his commission to

> A. B. Simpson's motto:
> "Take the whole Bible to the whole world."
>
> In 1882, Simpson started Nyack Missionary College in New York City, with the goal of training missionaries. Simpson was also engaged in inspiring all Christians to evangelize, and he felt a vehicle was needed to coordinate their finances, prayers, and gospel efforts for missions. Thus, the Christian and Missionary Alliance was founded.

carry the gospel to the multitudes, and he did so with relentless labor. He was careful to not err as some, who do nothing "because God will do all." Simpson professed, "I have been permitted by God to work—I say this to His honor." However, his work *for* Christ was accomplished by his communion *with* Christ:

> I used to be very fond of gardening. I could work in the garden and yet smell the roses.... They did not hinder the work a bit. So you can be busy all the time, and have the breath of heaven; it will not hinder you.... It is something deeper than prayer—[it is] communion.

Indeed, A. B. Simpson gained the "richer, sweeter" life of Christ by being crucified with Him:

> If I have ever done anyone any good, it was not I, but Christ in me.

Lord Jesus,

How real it is to me that I have been crucified with You—to the world, self, and sin. Thank You that holiness and strength do not depend on me, for You alone are holy and strong. You are my hope of glory! May Your death and resurrection become my continual reality.

Amen

I Am Crucified with Christ

Albert Benjamin Simpson
1843–1919

Albert Benjamin Simpson authored more than seventy books and many hymns and gospel songs. He founded the Christian and Missionary Alliance to send missionaries around the world. He established a publishing house, founded a college, and became a voice for Christian oneness to his generation.

December 15, 1843, on Prince Edward Island, A. B. Simpson was born to James and Jane Simpson. In 1865, he graduated from Knox College in Toronto and married Margaret Henry. They had six children. Despite the difficulties of obtaining a good education and suffering with serious health problems, Simpson became a Presbyterian minister and served congregations in Ontario, Kentucky, and New York.

But Simpson's heart of obedience to the Lord and his overwhelming burden to preach the gospel to the masses caused him to become stifled by and dissatisfied with the coldness and divisiveness found in the culture of formal Christianity. Simpson became burdened for two main matters: the gospel outreach to the world and the inner life experiences that most Christians were missing. Simpson became a beacon of light pointing believers to Christ and Christ alone.

Simpson learned how to live by resurrection life and how to maintain a moment-by-moment contact with the Lord. His "inbreathing of the very fullness of God" became his "daily renewal of life." Indeed, after spending several hours of fervent prayer for missionaries in Jamaica and abroad, he greeted the Lord in glory the following morning, Wednesday, October 29, 1919, at the age of seventy-six, having lived twice as long as doctors predicted.

I Am Crucified with Christ

Faithful Warrior

I WANT NOTHING FOR MYSELF;

I WANT EVERYTHING FOR THE LORD.

Watchman Nee

Conflict Today Is Fierce

Watchman Nee
1903–1972

FAITHFUL WARRIOR

〰〰✕✕✕〰〰

Finally, my brethren, be strong in the Lord and in the power of His might.
Put on the whole armor of God, that you may be
able to stand against the wiles of the devil. (Ephesians 6:10-11)

Watchman Nee had a keen awareness of the normally unseen war raging between God and Satan over the possession of mankind. As a voice declaring the truth concerning Christ in the spiritual darkness of China, Nee writes in this hymn how "hell's forces rally all their pow'rs" to stir up "the wildest storms." This war grows stronger, louder, harder, and more bitter toward the end.

If the truth of this hymn unmasks Satan's strategy to wear down and discourage God's people, it also works to awaken them from any confusion, numbness, and indifference toward the fight. Few Christians may ever be called to speak to thousands or suffer imprisonment for their faith as Nee did, but each one has an all-important opportunity to experience and display Christ's overcoming life in daily routines. We are surrounded by people who desperately need to see Him expressed through us. This is our battlefield until at last "the triumph song's begun!"

As soldiers in Christ's army, what should our attitude be toward this hidden, yet so real, war? Nee exhorts us to be encouraged, for the Lord Jesus quickly comes; to sing, for He is near; and to be happy, for we have greater power to witness. Captivated by His glorious return and motivated by the overcomers' future reward, we "will forward go, strong in His mighty power."

Conflict Today Is Fierce

Conflict Today Is Fierce

Verse One

Conflict today is fierce,
The strength of Satan more;
The cry of battle calling now
Is louder than before.
The rebel voice of hell
E'en stronger now becomes;
But list, the midnight cry resounds,
Behold, I quickly come!

Verse Two

Trials more bitter grow,
The fighting doth enlarge;
Hell's forces rally all their pow'rs
And gather for the charge.
Yet while we wait and watch
And feel the war severe,
We hear the joyful song ring out,
Jesus, the Lord, is near!

Verse Three

'Tis harder at the end
The word to testify,
For Satan fights with all his pow'r
Our witness to defy.
Much greater strength we need
The foe to overcome;
How happy when the Lord we see
And all our sighing's done!

Verse Four

Who then will forward go
Strong in His mighty power?
Who then will firmly trust the Lord
Until the vict'ry hour;
Till with the conqu'rors blest,
The triumph song's begun?
That man will then rejoice to hear,
Behold, I quickly come!

Verse Five

Who then will choose God's best,
And take the narrow track,
Though passing thru the wildest storms,
Yet never turning back?
Who now will dare press on,
Enduring pain and fear?
All such will then rejoice to see
Jesus, the Lord, is near!

Verse Six

Though deep the darkness be
We still would onward go,
Till we the day of rapture greet
And glory 'round shall glow.
'Tis there we'll see the Lord,
And Satan overcome;
The overcomers will rejoice,
Jesus, the Lord, has come!

CONFLICT TODAY IS FIERCE

Faithful Warrior

CROSSWINDS OF CHANGE

In the first half of the twentieth century, China was buffeted by turbulence from crosswinds of change. Controversy swirled on multiple fronts: political, economical, cultural, and religious.

The newly formed democratic government confronted ancient Chinese autocratic rule. Capitalism rivaled communist philosophy for the hearts and minds of the younger generation. The growth of Western influence endured bitter resistance from an ancient social culture that sought to keep China closed to the modern world. Buddhism's adherents challenged the advances of the Christian faith. It was an age of issues, questions, tensions, and clashes.

Even so, Watchman Nee had deeper insight concerning the apparent conflicts. Beneath the unstable surface, he saw that the real battle was between God and His enemy concerning this generation—at stake were the millions of souls in China and the testimony of Christ in this vast land.

*A*s night fell over the city of Foochow, China, spiritual conflict arose within the heart of seventeen-year-old Watchman Nee:

I experienced some mental conflict concerning whether or not to accept the Lord Jesus as my Savior and whether or not to become the Lord's servant.... At that time I was afraid of being saved, for I knew that once I was saved I must serve the Lord....

On the evening of April 29, 1920, I was alone in my room. I had no peace of mind.... My first inclination was not to believe in the Lord Jesus and not to be a Christian. However, that made me inwardly uneasy.... Then I knelt down to pray. At first I had no words with which to pray. But eventually many sins came before me, and I realized that I was a sinner.... I saw myself as a sinner and I also saw the Savior. I saw the filthiness of sin and I also saw the efficacy of the Lord's precious blood cleansing me.... I saw the Lord's hands nailed to the cross, and at the same time I saw Him stretching forth His arms to welcome me.... Overwhelmed by such love, I could not possibly reject it, and I decided to accept Him as my Savior.... I wept and confessed my sins, seeking the Lord's forgiveness. After making my confession, the burden of sins was discharged, and I felt buoyant and full of inward joy and peace.

Conflict Today Is Fierce

FROM AMBITION TO CONSECRATION

Prior to his birth, Nee had been consecrated to the Lord by his mother, who was a second-generation Christian. After giving birth to two girls, she bargained with the Lord, pleading, "If I have a boy, I will present him to You." Her petition was answered in 1903 when Watchman Nee was born. She could not have known how useful her consecrated gift would become to the Lord's work in China and beyond.

Nee was a gifted individual, possessing a photographic memory. Rarely studying for tests, he consistently made the highest grades. The teenage student knew that his future was bright, and he had ambitions to achieve both fame and fortune. Once saved, his ambitions previously devoted to worldly pursuits would now be directed toward serving Christ. However, despite his efforts to bring hundreds of classmates to Christ, he was not taken seriously!

Conflict Today Is Fierce

Through fellowship with Miss Groves, a missionary, he discovered the hindrance: "I immediately began to deal with my sins by making restitution, paying debts, being reconciled with my classmates.... Between 1920 and 1922, I went to at least two or three hundred people to confess offenses." Nee also began praying daily for his classmates, and soon all but one of the seventy students whose names were written in his notebook were saved.

However, Nee still longed to be "filled with the Holy Spirit to ... bring more people to the Lord." Due to his fellowship with Miss Margaret E. Barber, another missionary, Nee became convicted of a deeper matter between himself and the Lord. After a struggle, Nee felt that his love for an unbelieving girl named Charity Chang—the daughter of family friends

for three generations—had to be surrendered. He confessed, "When I spoke with her about the Lord Jesus and tried to persuade her to believe, she laughed at me. I must admit that I did love her, but at the same time I suffered her laughter at the Lord I believed in. I also questioned at that time whether she or the Lord would have first place in my heart."

One day ... Psalm 73:25 appeared before my eyes: "Whom have I in heaven but Thee? And there is none upon earth that I desire besides Thee." After reading these words I said to myself, "The writer of this psalm can say that, but I cannot."

The young man made every effort to distract himself from the Lord's word given to him concerning Charity. He related,

> Prior to Nee's salvation, he scoffed, *"I considered [preaching] the most trifling and base of occupations.... [Preachers] were servile subordinates to the missionaries and earned merely eight or nine dollars per month. I had no intention of becoming a preacher nor even a Christian."*
>
> However, after his salvation, he confessed,
> *"All my previous planning became void and was brought to nothing. My future career was entirely abandoned. For some this step might be easy, but for me,...it was exceedingly difficult."*

[I] asked God to be patient and impart strength to me until I could give her up. I asked God to postpone dealing with this matter. But God never reasons with people. I considered going to the frontier of desolate Tibet to evangelize and suggested many other enterprises to God, hoping that He might be moved not to raise again the question of my giving up the one I loved. But once God's finger has pointed to something, He will not withdraw it. No matter how I prayed, I could not get through. I prayed constantly, hoping that my earnest supplication might change God's mind.

Deeply convicted, Nee answered the Lord's call to "have none upon the earth" but Him. He later declared, "I was filled with His love, and I was willing to lay my loved one down." Obedience was followed by elation:

On that day I was in the second heaven, if not the third. The world appeared smaller to me, and it was as if I were mounting the clouds and riding the mists. On the evening of my salvation, the burden of my sins rolled away, but on that day, February 13, 1922, when I laid aside my beloved, my heart was emptied of everything that previously occupied me.

Soon, Nee and others expanded their gospel work, and "several hundred people were saved at the same time." Moreover, the earthly love Nee had previously crucified in his heart was now returned to him by the Lord in resurrection. After ten years, Charity also believed in Christ, and a new godly love was rekindled between them. They were married in 1934, and she proved to be the helpmate he needed.

LIVING BY FAITH

Throughout his life, Watchman Nee suffered from numerous physical ailments. At only twenty-one years of age, he contracted tuberculosis. He came so close to death that at

one point his doctor advised him to put his affairs in order, for he would not survive the night. Rumors circulated that he had already died. But by faith in God's Word, he was miraculously healed that evening, and all signs of the disease were forever gone. Nee believed that although his illness was an intense spiritual attack, it was allowed by God. While still seriously ill, he wrote, "What I have experienced during my illness is most profitable. From the very beginning I prayed that I would gain from this illness what I needed, for I am not willing to be ill for nothing."

Though miraculously healed from tuberculosis, God allowed a serious heart condition called *angina pectoris* to remain. For the rest of his life, he was constantly aware of his human frailty. Like Paul's thorn, which limited the gifted apostle, this unrelenting heart ailment sapped Nee's strength, causing him to rely on the Lord's grace. Often he was in great pain while sharing messages; breaking out into a sweat, he needed to lean against the podium in order to finish his speaking. Afterward, he could only lie in bed in pain. All during these physical trials, he affirmed the positive aspects of the circumstantial dealings in his life, saying that "a believer can never be the same after passing through suffering."

As one who lived by faith, Watchman Nee also had many experiences in trusting the Lord to meet his financial needs. In a message, he told

Conflict Today Is Fierce

this story concerning the Lord's provision of his traveling expenses while on a gospel journey:

When the time came for us to leave [for the provincial capital by bus], there was still no money in hand [for the ticket]. I packed my luggage as usual and hired a rickshaw.... When the rickshaw had been pulled about forty yards, an old man with a long gown came from behind shouting, "Mr. Nee, please stop!" ... After handing me a parcel of food as well as an envelope, the old man departed. I was then so grateful for God's arrangement that my eyes were filled with tears. When I opened the envelope, I found four dollars inside, just sufficient for a bus ticket.

He explained that he immediately sensed the devil's bothering him for trusting the Lord each step of the way:

The devil kept speaking to me, "Don't you see how dangerous it is?" I replied, "I was indeed a little anxious about it, but it is by no means dangerous, for God has supplied my need in time." After arriving in Amoy, another brother gave me a return ticket.

Framed quote in a Philippine meeting hall:

GOD PAYS ATTENTION MORE TO WHAT WE ARE THAN TO WHAT WE DO. THE REAL WORK IS THE OUTFLOW OF LIFE. THE SERVICE THAT COUNTS IS THE LIVING OUT OF CHRIST.

~ WN

He then concluded,

I can bear testimony today that God is the One Who gives.... It has been my experience that God's supply arrives when I have spent my last dollar. I have had fourteen years of experience. In each experience God wanted to get the glory for Himself. God has supplied all my needs and has not failed me once.

make himself rich. He was utterly captured by the Lord." Nee learned to endure with grace whatever came against him as he sought to advance God's purposes in China.

THE EFFECT OF THE CROSS

Watchman Nee renounced any self-seeking use of his natural talents in exchange for the life of a grain of wheat falling into the ground. He was convinced that the power of resurrection life carried out in godly service would be immensely more fruitful than his own power of persuasion. Thus, he encouraged others to live under the effect of the cross:

Nee learned how to accept God's sovereign circumstances and considered them as opportunities to gain Christ. For example, he developed successful companies solely consecrated for the financial support of Christian coworkers, the churches, and the Lord's work. While he was anonymously financing his fellow Christian servants, the very ones benefiting from his care started rumors that Nee had become worldly through working so hard at business. Nonetheless, he kept contributing to them while accepting their criticisms as from the Lord. Samuel Chang, Nee's brother-in-law, spoke concerning Nee's businesses: "I can bear witness that his motive was absolutely not to

Beloved brothers, the time of the Lord's coming back is fast approaching. We must be faithful. In the days ahead we may suffer more misunderstanding and more severe opposition; but since we have been destined for this we should remain faithful.... Brothers, please continue to remember me in your prayers so that in all my afflictions I may be able to stand fast, faithfully bearing a good testimony for the Lord.

Conflict Today Is Fierce

Watchman Nee refused the opportunity to flee China prior to the communist takeover in 1949. Rather, he chose to shepherd the flock there as long as he could. Consequently, he was imprisoned in 1952 and held unreasonably for years beyond his release date. Although it was his legal right, he was not allowed to visit his dying wife or attend her funeral. Furthermore, he was deprived of sufficient food and care, and thus he died an uncompromising martyr's death, true to the Lord after twenty years of imprisonment. A note written with shaking hand was found beneath his pillow and later quickly memorized by a family member who came to the prison after his death:

Christ is the Son of God Who died for the redemption of sinners and resurrected after three days. This is the greatest truth in the universe. I die because of my belief in Christ.

Lord Jesus,

Become the faithful One in me! Forgive my passivity in contending for the faith. Strengthen me to stand and be faithful to You until the end. You are the overcoming One in me. You are the Lord and God's Christ. How happy we will be at Your return! Come quickly, Lord Jesus!

Amen!

Watchman Nee
1903–1972

Watchman Nee was born as Nee Shu-tsu in Foochow, China, in 1903, into a third-generation Christian family. His paternal grandfather was the first Congregationalist pastor in northern Fukien province. His father studied in the American Methodist College in Foochow, and his mother was educated in the Chinese Western Girls' School in Shanghai.

Nee excelled at Anglican Trinity College in Foochow. After being saved in 1920, he adopted the English name Watchman Nee and the Chinese name *To-sheng,* meaning "the sound of a watchman's rattle." Through missionary Margaret E. Barber, he obtained the foundation of his spiritual life. In 1934, Watchman Nee married Charity Chang. They had no children.

Nee's preaching led to a spiritual revival in Foochow in 1923. Thereafter, he faithfully labored to minister the great truths of the Bible. He built a training center and held conferences for the perfecting of seeking believers. He financially supported Christian coworkers and needy saints. By 1949, he had been used in raising up hundreds of local churches—one in every major city of China's thirty-three provinces. Many of his messages have been compiled into book form, yielding a treasury of Christian literature. His writings and hymns continue to minister to Christians today.

His entire Christian life, Nee endured a steady battery of religious and political persecutions, culminating in imprisonment in 1952. Even so, he firmly maintained his overcoming testimony to the end. He died a martyr of Jesus Christ on May 30, 1972. Written just hours before he died, in shaking hand, are his final words:

I die because of my belief in Christ.

Captive Heart

Let us pray, my beloved, that God may

be made known and manifested to many hearts,

and thus in the light of

His divine presence the darkness of

mere human life may be dispelled.

Gerhardt Tersteegen

Something Ev'ry Heart Is Loving

GERHARDT TERSTEEGEN
1697–1769

CAPTIVE HEART

For it is the God who commanded light to shine out of darkness,
who has shone in our hearts to give the light of
the knowledge of the glory of God in the face of Jesus Christ. (2 Corinthians 4:6)

In a single glance, the eye can take in the loveliest beauty of creation and the worst degradation that society can offer. As shafts of light quickly penetrate the open eye to become vivid images in our consciousness, so the unguarded heart is an open door through which the whole world so easily enters the depths of our being. In this impressionable place, our very person within is continually influenced by the barrage of all that is without. The heart becomes the venue for blending all that occupies our being, both good and heavenly, or otherwise—what happens here determines who we are.

If the heart is a seeing organ, it is also a loving one, and every heart loves something. The heart whose primary love is found in its Creator is at rest. He is "beauteous more than all things beauteous." He is "loving, sweet, and tender." He is "full of pity, full of grace."

When the doors of our being are open to Him, His exposing and illuminating light shines in and brings with it a peace that presides over our heart. Yes, the peace of Christ acts as our heart's arbitrator to resolve its complications—to adjust and decide all things. In fact, single-hearted devotion to Christ opens up all the room in our heart for Him to make His home there. Thus, through His shining within, He initiates our transformation into a glorious reflection of His radiant face for others to see. May we guard our hearts above all earthly treasures since it has become the pursuit of Christ for His abode.

Something Ev'ry Heart Is Loving

Something Ev'ry Heart Is Loving

Verse One

Something ev'ry heart is loving:
If not Jesus, none can rest;
Lord, my heart to Thee is given;
Take it, for it loves Thee best.

Verse Two

Thus I cast the world behind me;
Jesus most beloved shall be;
Beauteous more than
   all things beauteous,
He alone is joy to me.

Verse Three

Bright with all eternal radiance
Is the glory of Thy face;
Thou art loving, sweet, and tender,
Full of pity, full of grace.

Verse Four

When I hated, Thou didst love me,
Shedd'st for me Thy precious blood;
Still Thou lovest, lovest ever,
Shall I not love Thee, my God?

Verse Five

Keep my heart still faithful to Thee,
That my earthly life may be
But a shadow to that glory
Of my hidden life in Thee.

SOMETHING EV'RY HEART IS LOVING

Captive Heart

WOUNDS OF WAR

The Thirty Years' War (1618–1648) ended with the Peace of Westphalia, but not before millions had died and once prospering cities had been decimated—wounds that would take two hundred years to heal. This pervasive bloodshed was not only a German civil war with political and religious underpinnings, but also a regional power struggle that at one time or another involved almost every western European nation.

As a result of the war, Germany remained mired in poverty, chaos, and social ruin the rest of the century. Furthermore, moral decay rippled throughout Europe, emanating from the licentious court of Louis XIV (1643–1715) in France. Concurrently, deep resentment grew in Europe due to France's frequent military campaigns and rising hegemony.

All of these cataclysmic events severely impacted the region of Westphalia in Germany where Tersteegen spent his life ministering Christ.

O how seldom we meet with those who are entirely God's, and yet how happy are such characters! The Lord willingly becomes their portion, their treasure, their all. That this may be the case with us is my sincerest wish.

≈ Gerhardt Tersteegen

By the end of Gerhardt Tersteegen's life, his wish—through God's abundant grace—had most assuredly been granted. The author of this beautiful and profound hymn "Something Ev'ry Heart Is Loving" was truly a rare and special vessel unto honor. His service was extraordinary; his story is unusual;

his testimony will endure. It is critical to see the significant strands woven together through the boy's experience to understand the fabric of the mature man.

SOVEREIGN HANDPRINTS ON A VESSEL OF MERCY

Tersteegen was born the youngest of eight children on November 25, 1697, in the German village of Mörs, near Düsseldorf, in the region of Westphalia. His father, Heinrich, a tradesman and an active member of the Reformed Church, died when Gerhardt was a young child, a portent of the path he would trek—one nearly devoid of connection with his family. He was frail and sickly as a youth, traits exacerbated by his particularly shy, sensitive, and introverted nature.

From the age of six to fifteen, young Gerhardt engrossed himself in the classical studies of Latin, Greek, Hebrew, and French, and excelled academically—early evidence of his prodigious talents, unusual conscientiousness, and self-discipline. But the loss of his father's income precluded the university education Gerhardt had hoped for. Instead, he was pressed into service in a dreary apprenticeship as a shopkeeper working for his brother-in-law, who in turn was so bothered by Gerhardt's brooding disposition that he forced him to push empty barrels in circles around the shop yard! In typical fashion, Tersteegen was later grateful that any exuberance of youth (not a noticeable attribute to begin with) was thus further curbed and abated. When he finished that apprenticeship, he left all family-related commerce and ran his own small business for two years, yet was repulsed by the busyness it necessarily required.

WE KNOW THAT GOD IS ALONE SUPREMELY GOOD. HE BEARS WITH ... HIS CHILDREN IN CHRIST, PREPARES THEM FOR THE ENJOYMENT OF HIMSELF WITH INCOMPREHENSIBLE CONDESCENSION AND LOVES THEM WITH PECULIAR TENDERNESS.

GT

In 1719, at age twenty-two, Gerhardt learned the simple skill of ribbon-weaving, which could be crafted in solitude. He had become certain that he must part ways with the desires of his family in order to be true to his insatiable desire to live alone and spend as much time as possible in prayer, study, and fasting.

In 1721, his mother, who was seemingly his sole sympathizer in the family, died. The rest of his family, experiencing increasing prosperity and ever more embarrassed by Gerhardt's menial job and altogether different path in life, scorned and derided him. In fact, their regard for him deteriorated to such an extent that when he fell under serious bouts of illness, they would not even suffer themselves to visit or attend to him in any way.

Thus, by both nature's course and family small-heartedness, he became truly isolated from his old hearth and home. However, he chose to respond in love and with forgiveness instead of harboring bitterness when his family misunderstood his manner of service to God.

In fact, Gerhardt *preferred* his new life: "How happy I was when I found myself living all alone! I often thought no king in the whole world could be as fully contented as I was."

With the Scriptures as his companion, he wove ribbons from five in the morning to nine at night, and saw no one except a servant girl who would bring him food. His preferred diet was one meal per day of flour, water, and milk. Why? Mainly to save money to give all he could to the poor. Sometimes he would fast, pray, and study through the night.

The sharp-edged extremes—his fragile health, his family's rejection, his brooding introspection, his iron self-will, his great intellect, his delicate conscience, his monastic self-sacrifice, and his total isolation—all combined to chisel away at Tersteegen to a breaking point, and he did!

Tersteegen's seclusion and asceticism produced a "state of darkness," both physical and spiritual, that lasted more than five years. Yet, he was not spiritually without a friend on earth. Over the years, he had been looked after by Wilhelm Hoffman, who was his enduring spiritual mentor. In earlier years, Tersteegen had been a regular attendee at Hoffman's prayer meetings. But during the sustained dark period, he felt cut off from the love of Christ to such an extent that he began to doubt his faith.

Full of Pity; Full of Grace

At last, in the spring of 1724, light broke upon Tersteegen. One day he was walking through the woods to Duisburg on business when he became violently ill. At only twenty-seven, he felt that he was going to die and, in his agony, asked the Lord to give him some time to get ready. The title of the hymn he was writing during that period of his life accurately expressed this cry: "Jesus, Pitying Savior, Hear Me." On that trip, the Spirit, Who had been working in his spirit and spreading into his heart, empowered even his earthly body. The pain went away, and he gave himself unreservedly to God. The next morning, "the glory and the sweetness of the love of God poured into his soul as a flood of light from the innermost heaven." He was so overcome with joy that he immediately composed a poem containing the following verse:

No more my countless sins shall rise
To fill me with dismay—
That precious blood before His eyes,
Hath put them all away.

The cry Tersteegen had uttered before his newfound freedom had been answered by the One Who is "full of pity, full of grace." At long last, he had been "led out of the horror of the great darkness of the law by Christ Himself." In that same spring, he wrote a formal covenant to God:

MY JESUS,—I own myself to be Thine, my only Saviour and Bridegroom, Christ Jesus. I am Thine wholly and eternally. I renounce from my heart all right and authority that Satan unrighteously gave me over myself, from this evening henceforward.

On this evening—the evening when Thou, my Bridegroom through the precious blood, ... didst purchase me for Thyself, agonizing even unto death, praying till Thy sweat was as blood falling to the ground, that I might be Thy treasure and Thy bride, ... my heart and all my love are offered up to Thee in eternal thankfulness.

From this evening to all eternity, Thy will, not mine, be done. Command, and rule, and reign in me. I yield myself up without reserve.... Behold Thou hast me wholly and completely, sweet Friend of my soul. Thou hast the love of my heart for Thyself, and for none other. Thy Spirit be my keeper....

Thine unworthy possession,
GERHARDT TERSTEEGEN.

RECLUSE IN DEMAND

God wrought dramatic changes in Tersteegen's heart. Self-striving was replaced with the grace of Christ. The desire for solitude was displaced by a growing delight in caring for others and was tempered by the fellowship and support of Heinrich Sommer, who came to reside with Tersteegen and work as his apprentice. With Sommer's help, Tersteegen spent more time in biblical and medical studies, the latter arising from his keen desire to minister not only to the spiritual, but also to the physical needs of others.

He started and maintained an ever-expanding "book of remembrance" for daily intercessory prayer. In addition, he increased his labors in translating the historical writings of those who had particularly pursued the subjective experience of Christ. Moreover, he compiled a book of hymns to enrich corporate worship and praise, and he began to speak at Hoffman's meetings. Three short years later, when Tersteegen was thirty, the region was in spiritual revival—there was no more time for ribbon-weaving!

Tersteegen's ministry of Christ attracted ever-increasing numbers—many from other countries—which swelled to overflowing crowds. He would minister Christ through the Scriptures and give counsel to individuals or groups of "ten, twenty, even thirty anxious souls." He affirmed each and every measure of consecration to Christ:

It is impossible for me to see with indifferent or unappreciative eyes the smallest, weakest, most faulty beginning of a course, in which a single soul ... is pressing forward to live out the life of Jesus.

In light of his strong predisposition to solitary reflection, he had to yield to the Lord in greater measure to allow Christ to shine to the throngs. Later, upon moving into a larger home that afforded a medical clinic and meeting place, he would spend the rest of his life ministering from dawn to dusk, in health or infirmities, surrounded by as many as four hundred people.

Tersteegen would not affiliate with one faction of Christ's church at the exclusion of another. He was unequivocal on the matter; indeed, his heart was grieved by religious divisions, particularly new ones. When asked what religion people were who came to him, he replied, "I ask not whence they come, but whither they are going."

"Something Ev'ry Heart Is Loving"

Beauteous More than All Things Beauteous

Gerhardt Tersteegen knew the human heart must always be attached to *something*, whether to Christ or to the world. Seeing Christ as the One Who is "beauteous more than all things beauteous" compelled him to share the profoundly simple secret to living the Christian life:

The secret of God's presence is actually believed by very few. But are you aware, that if each one truly believed it, the whole world would at once be filled with saints, and the earth would be truly Paradise? If men really believed it as they should, [they] would need nothing more to induce them to give themselves up, heart and soul, to this loving God. But now it is hid from their eyes.

Let us pray, my beloved, that God may be made known and manifested to many hearts, and thus in the light of His divine presence the darkness of mere human life may be dispelled, and all things cast away, both without and within the heart, which hinder the growth and

It is a matter of astonishment, adoration, and delight, to see how the Lord can induce us to let every thing go. Everything appears so frivolous, unsatisfying, trifling, and superficial—even good and spiritual things which formerly afforded such gratification and of which we were so tenacious, but which, for that very reason, served only to interpose between us and God, and were injurious, because they were held so fast. *Jesus alone is sufficient, but yet insufficient, when He is not wholly and solely embraced.*

— GT

life of the soul, and which this light alone discovers and unveils.

In all Christian practice there is nothing more universally needful, nothing simpler, sweeter, and more useful, nothing which so sums up in itself all

"Something Ev'ry Heart Is Loving"

131

Christian duties in one blessed act, as the realization of the loving presence of God.

Accordingly, let us gaze into the glory of the Lord Jesus' face! We will disdain and thus cast the world behind us, for "Jesus most beloved shall be." Day by day, He alone will keep our heart faithful, proving that our earthly life is "but a shadow to that glory" of our "hidden life" in Him! "Something Ev'ry Heart Is Loving" reveals the intimate relationship Gerhardt Tersteegen enjoyed as he peered into the radiant face of Christ—the same loving, sweet, and tender face we may also seek today. More than two centuries ago, he affirmed so tenderly:

He alone is joy to me.

Lord Jesus,

How radiant You are to me! How You have loved me so sweetly, so tenderly, even when I hated! You are full of pity for my helpless condition. You are full of grace to take me through each day. Thank You for shedding Your precious blood for me. In spite of my changeable feelings, Lord, my heart truly loves You best. I offer my heart to You today, knowing that You alone can keep it faithful for eternity. Continually show me how real the fact is that my earthly life is only a shadow when compared to the glory of Your hidden life in me. I love You, Lord Jesus!

Amen!

Something Ev'ry Heart Is Loving

Gerhardt Tersteegen
1697–1769

Gerhardt Tersteegen was born in Germany on November 25, 1697, amid the residual strife of the Thirty Years' War. His father, Heinrich, who had been a merchant, died when Gerhardt was only six years old, thus reducing his station in life. Heinrich had been a devout Christian, but his early death precluded his ability to imprint his son with his Christian example. Young Gerhardt studied diligently at the local Latin school for nine years, looking forward to attending university, only to find out that his mother did not have the means to fulfill his wish after all.

Consequently, at age fifteen, Gerhardt found himself apprenticed to his brother-in-law in Muhlheim—in a menial trade he disliked. However, in the next five years, he enjoyed a flourishing spiritual revival in the city. Thus, he was brought to Christ through the shepherding of Wilhelm Hoffman, who held weekly prayer meetings.

Tersteegen took up ribbon-weaving and lived an isolated, ascetic life, which eventually led to five years of depression and darkness. After being gloriously set free, he possessed a much greater understanding of God's grace. Hoffman later helped Tersteegen by convincing him to live a less isolated lifestyle. Tersteegen took on an apprentice to help him, thus giving him more time to speak publicly.

What followed was a lifetime of ministering to the Body of Christ! This unceasing labor for almost forty-six years took a toll on his health, causing him grave illness in 1758. He spent his remaining eleven years completing 111 hymns and publishing devotional writings, poems, and sermons. He served as strength allowed until his death on April 3, 1769.

Something Ev'ry Heart Is Loving

Consecration

 KEEP YOUR HEART WITH ALL DILIGENCE,

FOR OUT OF IT SPRING

THE ISSUES OF LIFE. *Proverbs 4:23*

Lord, Keep My Heart

HOWARD HIGASHI
1937–1998

CONSECRATION

Now hope does not disappoint, because the love of God has been poured out in our hearts by the Holy Spirit who was given to us. (Romans 5:5)

But we all, with unveiled face, beholding as in a mirror the glory of the Lord, are being transformed into the same image from glory to glory, just as by the Spirit of the Lord. (2 Corinthians 3:18)

In nature, the sun's rays cause a plant to lift its leaves directly toward its source of life. It is the sunlight itself that stimulates life in the plant. Likewise, our hearts were created to respond to God's light. When God, through His great mercy, shines into our hearts, we respond in consecration to Him. Hence, the Christian heart is a God-kindled heart.

Nevertheless, God has committed to us the stewardship of our hearts, which left unguarded become frustrated by the many worldly distractions and busyness of daily life. But when protected, our hearts become conduits through which Christ Himself may flow as the spring of life.

We are presented a paradox—God requires us to guard our hearts, but we quickly sense our inability to do so! We are compelled to cry out, as Howard Higashi did in this song, "Lord, keep my heart!" Thus, we guard our hearts by committing them to His loving keep. How wonderful that we may completely trust the Son of God, Who is not only able, but also sweetly willing, to hear and answer our earnest prayers.

God is both Light and Love! Through His shining into us, He unveils, enlivens, and seals our hearts. By the pouring out of His love into our hearts, we are softened and opened to the Life-giver. Thus mercifully filled by God, we willingly consecrate our lives afresh to Him, and Christ is daily formed in us, making His home in our hearts.

Lord, Keep My Heart

Lord, Keep My Heart

Verse One

Lord, keep my heart always true to You,
Never backsliding, always viewing You,
A heart that is pure, that sees only You,
A heart that loves You and
   treasures only You.

Verse Two

Lord, keep my love burning
   brightly for You,
A love never dwindling, always
   hot for You,
A love, shining brighter all
   the way for You,
A love so fresh, like the day
   I first touched You.

Chorus:

Your love constrains me to
   give my all to You!
Lord, I can't help it; my heart
   is drawn to You!
Oh, what a privilege!
   I give myself to You!
I love You, Lord, dearest Lord,
I love You! I just love You!

Verse Three

Lord, take my life; I present it to You!
If I had a thousand, I'd pour all on You!
Nothing withholding; my all is for You:
My life and my future, dear Lord,
   are all for You.

Consecration

LORD, KEEP MY HEART

Consecration

A CAPTURED HEART

The spiritual song "Lord, Keep My Heart" was spontaneously composed by Howard Higashi while singing to the Lord. It is a transparent, intimate prayer offered from a consecrated heart. This prayer in song is addressed directly to the Lord, the last word of every line ending with "You." These genuine utterances flow from one who was immersed in God's Word. The Scriptures became both the author's active vocabulary with which to articulate his requests to God and the heavenly energy that caused his love relationship with Jesus to burn. We invite you to look into and lay hold of the spiritual wealth within these prayers—and to make these requests your very own.

THE HEART GOD DESIRES

On a tempestuous sea, the Lord beckoned to His disciple Peter, "Come." Peter eagerly leaped from the storm-tossed boat and walked over surging waves to be in the presence of the Lord Jesus. Even though the wind and waves were beating against him, Peter could not sink as long as his eyes were fixed on Jesus. But in fear of the surging waves, he glanced away from Jesus' face—just for a moment—and he instantly began to sink. He cried out, "Lord, save me!" The Savior immediately stretched out His hand, took hold of Peter, and brought him safely into the boat.

The heart that God desires is a *pure* heart, one solely directed toward Him. We must ask the Lord to keep our hearts true, "never backsliding," and "always viewing" the Savior we hold precious. Every heart is prone to wander from God, every eye to see and fear the storms of life; therefore, like Peter, we must keep "looking unto Jesus" to be kept from sinking.

THE LOVE GOD DESIRES

Sometime later, Peter uttered his dreadful denials—denials that began by his following the Lord Jesus *at a distance*. Then, by the time the mockers' accusations came, Peter denied even knowing the Lord. One look from Jesus melted him, and he went out and wept bitter tears. But later, the Lord Jesus tenderly guided Peter to replace his three denials with three proclamations of love, by asking him, "Do you love Me?" The more we profess that we love Jesus—even when our feelings protest it isn't so—the less we live a life of denying Him. The heart that God desires is a *loving* heart, and we pray for a "love burning brightly ... never dwin-

dling." This song gives opportunity to echo the words of the oft-failing, oft-repenting, and *oft-comforted* Peter, "Yes, Lord ... I love You!"

THE LIFE GOD DESIRES

In the temple, the Lord was moved by a poor widow withholding nothing in her giving. He turned to His disciples and appraised her offering in this way:

Assuredly, I say to you that this poor widow has put in more than all those who have given to the treasury; for they all put in out of their abundance, but she out of her poverty put in all that she had, her whole livelihood. (Mark 12:43–44)

THEN MARY TOOK A POUND OF VERY COSTLY OIL OF SPIKENARD, ANOINTED THE FEET OF JESUS, AND WIPED HIS FEET WITH HER HAIR. AND THE HOUSE WAS FILLED WITH THE FRAGRANCE OF THE OIL. (JOHN 12:3)

THROUGHOUT THE CENTURIES, LOVERS OF CHRIST HAVE POURED OUT BRIGHT FUTURES AND HEART-TREASURES ON HIM. LIKE MARY, THEY HAVE ALWAYS HAD THEIR ANTAGONISTS RISING UP TO PROTEST, "WHY THIS WASTE?" UNDETERRED, THEY LOVINGLY RESPOND, AS MARY DID, BY GIVING THEIR ALL TO THE SAVIOR.

The Lord's standard of measure was not according to the amount, but to the extent of her sacrifice, which was at great personal cost. The life the Lord desires is one of *absolute surrender*. "Nothing withholding" yields a fragrant

and spontaneous response from a heart compelled to love Him. And we cannot help but love Him, for He is so lovely!

LORD, KEEP MY HEART

God's divine love is utterly tender to us, but fiercely protective of our fidelity to Himself. Therefore, He tells us, "Keep yourselves in the love of God, looking for the mercy of our Lord Jesus Christ unto eternal life" (Jude 21). Indeed, God sovereignly arranges our circumstances so that we will find His mercy, whether in being preserved through life's storms, tenderly shepherded back from denials and coldness, or encouraged in sacrifice. Our hearts are kept from falling by continually opening to our love-filling God; thus, we may simply follow the pattern of these dear ones who declared by their words and actions, "Lord Jesus, I love You!"

Lord Jesus,

Keep my heart always true to You. Keep my love burning brightly for You. I present my life to You even now, once again, yielding all into Your hands. You alone are worthy of my heart, my love, and my life.

Amen

BIBLIOGRAPHY AND ACKNOWLEDGMENTS

Scripture quotations are from *The New King James Version*. Copyright © 1979, 1980, 1982, Thomas Nelson, Inc., Publishers.

Hidden Pearls gratefully acknowledges Stan Moser for his continual guidance and support toward *Hidden Pearls*, as well as Toni Fitzpenn of Venture Publications for her artistic vision and direction throughout the production of *Come and Rejoice*.

"Come and Rejoice with Me" by Elisabeth Rundle Charles

Charles, Elisabeth Rundle. *Our Seven Homes*. (An autobiography.) London: John Murray, 1896.

Family Search Database. www.familysearch.org (for genealogy records; accessed October 10, 2003).

Hustad, Donald P. *Dictionary-Handbook to Hymns for the Living Church*. Carol Stream, IL: Hope Publishing Company, 1978.

McCutchan, Robert Guy. *Our Hymnody*. 2nd ed. New York: Abingdon-Cokesbury Press, 1937.

"O Christ, He Is the Fountain" by Anne Ross Cousin

Beattie, David J. *Stories and Sketches of Our Hymns and Their Writers*. Kilmarnock, Scotland: John Ritchie, Publishers of Christian Literature, 1934.

Bonar, Andrew A., ed. *Letters of Samuel Rutherford: With a Sketch of His Life and Biographical Notices of His Correspondents*. Edinburgh: Oliphant Anderson & Ferrier, 1891.

Cassells, David. "Samuel Rutherford of Fair Anworth." http://www.banneroftruth.org/pages/articles/article_detail.php?356.

Houghton, Elsie. *Classic Christian Hymn-Writers*. Fort Washington, PA: Christian Literature Crusade, 1992.

Pitt, F. W. *The Romance of Women Hymn Writers*. Findlay, OH: Fundamental Truth Publishers, n.d.

Rendell, Kingsley G. *Samuel Rutherford: A New Biography of the Man & His Ministry*. Fearn, Scotland: Christian Focus Publications, 2003.

Ross, Neil M. "Samuel Rutherford." Paper presented to the 2001 Free Presbyterian Theological Conference. *Free Presbyterian Magazine*, December 2002, January 2003, February 2003, March 2003, April 2003. http://home.rednet.co.uk/homepages/fpchurch/EbBI/index.htm.

Smith, Wilbur M., and S. Maxwell Coder, eds. *The Letters of Samuel Rutherford*. Chicago: Moody Press, 1951.

Whyte, Alexander. *Samuel Rutherford and Some of His Correspondents*. Edinburgh: Oliphant Anderson & Ferrier, 1894. http://www.puritansermons.com/ruth/ruthindx.htm.

"I Cannot Breathe Enough of Thee" by William Spencer Walton

Brain, Robert Wesley. "History of the South Africa General Mission." A dissertation presented to the faculty of the Graduate School: Gordon Divinity School. December 1953.

Weeks, George E. *W. Spencer Walton: Approved of God to Be Intrusted with the Gospel*. London: Marshall Brothers, 1907.

"And Can It Be?" by Charles Wesley

Dallimore, Arnold A. *A Heart Set Free: The Life of Charles Wesley*. Westchester, IL: Crossway Books, 1988.

Mitchell, T. Crichton. *Charles Wesley: Man with the Dancing Heart*. Kansas City: Beacon Hill Press, 1994.

Tyson, John R., ed. *Charles Wesley: A Reader*. Oxford: Oxford University Press, 1989.

Image of the Holy Club reproduced by courtesy of John Wesley: Holiness of Heart and Life Web site. http://gbgm-umc.org/umw/wesley/.

Image of Wesley reproduced by courtesy of the Director and Librarian, the John Rylands University Library of Manchester.

"Where Is He, My Jesus?" by Howard Higashi

© 2000 Living Stream Ministry, Anaheim, CA USA Used by Permission. All Rights Reserved. International Copyright Secured.

Charles, Elisabeth Rundle. *Songs Old and New*. London: Society for Promoting Christian Knowledge, 1894.

Higashi Family, Friends, and Co-Workers. Transcription of unpublished interviews. January 2001.

Hidden Pearls gratefully acknowledges the family of Howard Higashi for their assistance and the provision of photos.

"Satisfied" by Clara Tear Williams

Cartwright, Peter. *Autobiography of Peter Cartwright: The Backwoods Preacher*. New York: Nelson & Phillips, 1856.

Simpson, Robert. "The Circuit-Riders in Early American Methodism." http://www.gcah.org/Circuit_Riders.html.

Williams, Clara Tear. "Life of Clara Tear Williams." Unpublished Autobiography, Houghton College Library, New York.

Hidden Pearls gratefully acknowledges the family of Clara Tear Williams for their assistance and the provision of photos.

"I Am Crucified with Christ" by A.B. Simpson

Thompson, A.E. *A.B. Simpson: His Life and Work*. Camp Hill, PA: Christian Publications, 1960.

Tozer, A.W. *Wingspread: Albert B. Simpson–A Study in Spiritual Altitude*. Harrisburg, PA: Christian Publications, 1943.

Image of Simpson reproduced by courtesy of The Christian & Missionary Alliance National Archives.

"Conflict Today Is Fierce" by Watchman Nee

© 1966 Living Stream Ministry, Anaheim, CA USA Used by Permission. All Rights Reserved. International Copyright Secured.

Lee, Witness. *Watchman Nee: A Seer of the Divine Revelation in the Present Age*. Anaheim, CA: Living Stream Ministry, 1997.

Images reproduced by courtesy of Living Stream Ministry, Anaheim, CA.

"Something Ev'ry Heart Is Loving" by Gerhardt Tersteegen

Bevan, Frances. *Sketches of the Quiet in the Land*. London: John F. Shaw, n.d.

Harvey, Lillian G., ed. *Recluse in Demand: Gerhard Tersteegen, Life and Letters*. Shoals, IN: Old Paths Tract Society, 1990.

New Schaff-Herzog Encyclopedia of Religious Knowledge, s.v. "Tersteegen, Gerhard," http://www.ccel.org/php/disp.php3?a=schaff&b=encyc11&p=304 (accessed August 12, 2003).

Hidden Pearls gratefully acknowledges Trudy Tait of Harvey Christian Publishers for her assistance in the preparation of this chapter.

Image of Tersteegen reproduced by courtesy of Tersteegen Haus, Muhlheim, Germany.

"Lord, Keep My Heart" by Howard Higashi

© 2000 Living Stream Ministry, Anaheim, CA USA Used by Permission. All Rights Reserved. International Copyright Secured.

Higashi Family, Friends, and Co-Workers. Transcription of unpublished interviews. January 2001.

Hidden Pearls gratefully acknowledges the family of Howard Higashi for their assistance and the provision of photos.

Hidden Pearls gratefully acknowledges the assistance of Carl P. Daw Jr. of *The Hymn Society;* and Mary Louise VanDyke of *The Dictionary of North American Hymnology*, Oberlin College Library.

Hidden Pearls—Come and Rejoice CD

Companion Choral CD

Recording Credits

Executive Producer – James G. Waldrup III
Associate Executive Producers – Brad D. Brown and Virginia M. Davis
Produced by Dick Tunney
Additional Choral Production – Brian and Sharon Felten

Recording engineers – Brent King, Dick Tunney, Bob Clark
Remix engineer – Brent King
Mastering – Hank Williams/MasterMix

Orchestra recorded at Angel Studios (London, England), Sony Music Studios, (London, England)
Choral vocals recorded at TransContinental Studios (Orlando, Florida),
Gaither Studios (Alexandria, Indiana), Dream In Color Studio (Brentwood, Tennessee)
Additional recording – Dream In Color Studio (Brentwood, Tennessee), Sound Kitchen (Brentwood, Tennessee),
OmniSound Recording (Nashville, Tennessee), Quad Studios (Nashville, Tennessee) Ocean Way (Nashville, Tennessee),
Mixed at Dream In Color Studio (Brentwood, Tennessee)

Orchestra – The London Philharmonic Orchestra, Robert St. James Wright, Concertmaster
Orchestra conductors – Tom Keene, Dick Tunney
Additional percussion – Eric Darken
Piano, Accordian – Dick Tunney
Guitar – David Cleveland
Bass – Craig Nelson
Pennywhistle, Irish flute – Sam Levine
Bantar, Mandolin – Tom Keene
Additional strings, String quartet – The Nashville String Machine

Arrangers:

Come and Rejoice with Me – Don Hart
O Christ, He Is the Fountain – Doug Schoen
I Cannot Breathe Enough of Thee – Doug Schoen
And Can It Be? – Don Hart
Deep into the Depths *(edited instrumental version)* – Don Hart
Where Is He, My Jesus? – Dan Galbraith
Satisfied – Doug Schoen
I Am Crucified With Christ – Tom Keene
From Prayer That Asks *(edited instrumental version)* – Tom Keene
Conflict Today Is Fierce – Jerry Nelson
Something Ev'ry Heart Is Loving – Doug Schoen
Lord, Keep My Heart – Don Hart

Singers

Michelle Amato, Tammy Boyer, Amy Martin Cole, Travis Cottrell, Lisa De Haan
Tony DeRosa, Brian Felten, Rod Fletcher, Mary Bates George, Stephanie Hall, Marshall Hall, Margaret Harden
Bryan Harden, Shelley Harris, Paul Langford, Michelle Lindau, Karyn List, Shane McConnell
Shelley Nirider, Denise Pitzer, Lana Ranahan, Kelly Roth, Amy Rouse, Jane Sherberg, Jon Sherberg, Felicia Starkes
Leah Taylor, Brock Thornsborough, Kurt vonSchmittou

COME! COME AND REJOICE
WITH US IN SONG!

The Perfect Gift

Give the gift of powerful and glorious music
in this recording of joyous voices singing hymns and spiritual songs
with the London Philharmonic Orchestra.

Hidden Pearls—Come and Rejoice is available in choral and instrumental versions.

Experience these *pearls of great worth*
in song and make their joyful response your own.

Visit www.hiddenpearls.com for the latest product news.

Additional information, anecdotes, and devotional insight about each author
in *Come and Rejoice* can be found on our Web site. Also, enjoy more inspirational music
by listening to *Hidden Pearls Radio*—all at hiddenpearls.com.

Companion Compact Discs are available
through your local retailer or at www.hiddenpearls.com.

HIDDEN PEARLS